GW01607209

THE POEMS AND SELECTED LETTERS OF

CHARLES HAMILTON SORLEY

CHARLES HAMILTON SORLEY

THE POEMS AND SELECTED LETTERS OF

Charles Hamilton Sorley

edited with an introduction and notes by

Hilda D. Spear

Preface by

The Rt. Hon. Lord Butler, KG., CH.

For Andrew – a better copy.

With best wishes

Hilda D. Spear.

BLACKNESS PRESS

1978

First published in 1978 by Blackness Press

Paperback: ISBN 0 906292 00 X
Hardback: ISBN 0 906292 01 8

Cover drawing by David Millar

The publisher acknowledges the financial assistance of the Scottish Arts Council in the publication of this volume.

Printed in Great Britain by G.G. Stevenson (Printers) Ltd., Dundee

To

MY FATHER

who also served in the Great War

ACKNOWLEDGMENTS

For his interest, help and encouragement in all things to do with Sorley I should like to thank Mr. Gerald W. Murray, Librarian of Marlborough College. Thanks are also due to my Honours students at Dundee University from 1973 to 1978 who have discussed with me the work of Sorley and other writers of the Great War. For help and kindness in various ways I should also like to thank the late Mrs. Jean Bickersteth, the late Mr. Kenneth Sorley, Mr. Joseph Bain, Mrs. Moira Anthony and Mr. G.G. Stevenson. I should also like to express my gratitude to the Scottish Arts Council for their interest in the re-publishing of Sorley's work and for financial assistance.

CONTENTS

PREFACE

by The Rt. Hon. Lord Butler, KG., CH.

Charles Sorley's mother, Janetta, was my mother's sister. She was very gay and wrote a book about Cambridge which reflected some of Charlie's wit. His father was dour and Knightbridge Professor of Philosophy at King's College, Cambridge. He wrote very slowly and his chief book is *Moral Values and the Idea of God.* He was a sombre man. The traits he inherited from his mother and father are reflected in Sorley's poems. The early ones about Marlborough and the Downs are lighter and gayer than the later grim forebodings of the war and of death.

Charlie was killed leading his company at Loos, being shot in the head by a sniper. Robert Graves, who has always been an admirer, wrote as follows:

> 'Gradually the noise died down and at last a message came from the brigade that we would not be needed. It had been another dud show, chiefly notorious for the death of Charles Sorley, a twenty-year old captain in the Suffolks, one of the three poets of importance killed during the war.'

The other two being Isaac Rosenberg and Wilfred Owen. The latter two were, of course, far more mature than Sorley and this is reflected in their poetry. They also saw much more of the war and were not killed at the outset.

Robert Graves writes in some of his other poems about Sorley's rain. Charlie used to love running on the Downs in the rain and he asked where people found their God and goes on to say, 'In the rain where I found mine'. There was a battered signpost past which he used to run and which has since been renovated in a ceremony to commemorate his memory. He used to run as far as Barbury Camp and he admired the ramparts built by the Romans. Poems nearer home were 'East Kennet Church at Evening':

For now no church nor tree nor fold
Was visible to me:
Only that fading into one
Which God must sometimes see.

He also wrote about rooks:

Still trouble all the trees with cries
That know, and cannot put away,
The yearning to the soul that flies
From day to night, from night to day.

and he confessed that he was bound to them

By bondage tighter, tenderer
Than any lovers ever were.

He wrote about the river, but above all of the Downs.

After gaining a scholarship to Oxford he went to Germany and his *Letters from Germany and from the Army* constituted perhaps the most striking example of his growing maturity. He was a voracious reader, in English of Hardy and Masefield, and in Greek of the Odyssey. He wrote to his parents, 'it is a great joy when once you read it in big chunks' and he compared certain aspects of Homeric Greece to the Germany of 1914. He enjoyed Germany and his hosts and that is why the war came as such a cruel blow to him. He wrote about Germany:

You are blind like us. Your hurt no man designed,
And no man claimed the conquest of your land.
But gropers both through fields of thought confined
We stumble and we do not understand.

Before he died he wrote 'Expectans Expectavi':

This sanctuary of my soul
Unwitting I keep white and whole
Unlatched and lit, if Thou should'st care
To enter or to tarry there.

This has been sung as an anthem at King's College Chapel, Cambridge, and at Westminster Abbey.

It is impossible to say what future Charlie would have had after taking up his scholarship. Some say he would have taken to social work and others that he would have been a dramatist. At any rate England lost a poet.

February 1978

INTRODUCTION

Charles Hamilton Sorley was killed in the Battle of Loos on the 13th of October 1915. He was twenty years old and on the threshold of life. In July 1914 the world was before him; in August 1914 it had fallen about his ears: 'But isn't all this bloody?' he wrote to a schoolfriend, 'I am full of mute and burning rage and annoyance and sulkiness about it' (see page 91)

Sorley was born the elder of twin boys in Don Street, Old Aberdeen, on the 19th of May 1895. Now owned by the university, the house stands within the university precincts, but bears no commemorative plaque. His father, William Ritchie Sorley, was Professor of Moral Philosophy at the university at the time of Charles's birth and from him Charles learned his contemplative attitude to life. Mrs. Sorley was an imaginative and cultured woman who inherited a love of books and reading, from her father, George Smith, the Edinburgh journalist and writer. This love she passed on to her own children, Charles and his twin brother Kenneth and their older sister Jean, reading to them and telling them stories, developing their imaginations from the moment they were able to respond to the sound of words.

Charles's earliest memories were of the Aberdeenshire countryside and seashore; he would have watched the herons fishing in the Don and heard the strange cry of the curlews on the moors, but it was not by them that he was moved. However, the loneliness and independence of the countryside, the vastness and often frightening aspects of the seascapes made a lasting impression upon the boy and seem to have influenced his whole way of thinking about man and nature, so that, as he grew up, he was attracted, not by the sentimental and romanticized aspects of nature, the sun, the birds, the flowers, but by the independent and unfettered wildness of rain and wind and by the enduring character of the earth itself.

When the twins were five years old their father was appointed Knightbridge Professor of Moral Sciences at the University of

Cambridge and the family moved south. Though Charles returned to Scotland on visits to his relations he quickly ceased to think of himself as a Scot; he appeared to make a complete imaginative break with the country of his birth and his poetry rarely reminds us overtly of his Scottish heritage, though in his letters he occasionally lays claim to Scottish characteristics. The flat and mellow countryside around Cambridge never really attracted him, however; for some years he attended King's College Choir School as a day-boy; there he was happy and successful and comparatively contented with his lot, but Cambridgeshire failed to capture his imagination. Then, in 1908, he won a scholarship to Marlborough College and there, at the age of thirteen, he found his true sense of belonging. The Wiltshire Downs became a spiritual home to him, perhaps calling up deep from his childhood memories the loneliness and largeness, the bleakness and windy aspect of the countryside around Aberdeen:

Wind, that has blown here always ceaselessly,
Bringing, if any man can understand,
Might to the mighty, freedom to the free;
Wind, that has caught us, cleansed us, made us grand,
Wind that is we...

He found an affinity for the Wiltshire countryside which he had never experienced in Cambridgeshire. After he had left school his nostalgia was not for Aberdeen, nor for Cambridge, but for Wiltshire, 'I know it's wrong of me,' he wrote to the Master of Marlborough in July 1914, 'but I count myself as Wiltshire'.

At Marlborough, Charles blossomed and flourished; he threw himself into the life of the school both at work and at play. He was a competent classicist and worked well at his Greek, but Latin did not appeal to him. His main intellectual interest was in English literature and he read widely, boldly summing up and making his own judgements, though they were often immature and perhaps sometimes ill-informed. He had the independence and self-confidence to address the school Literary Society on a number of occasions, first on established nineteenth century writers and then, more originally, on contemporary figures—John Masefield and A. E. Housman. At the age of seventeen he was a rigorous and fearless critic; he had already learned that the first job of a critic is to read and know the work he is writing about, and the second is to look at specific aspects of the work, not to write in broad generalisations. His unbridled admiration for Masefield was perhaps a youthful excess, just as was his extravagant dislike of the Victorians, particularly Tennyson and Browning, but at least he nurtured an independence of judgment based on a careful study of the works he had read.

His interests, however, were by no means solely academic. He was a keen member of the school's O.T.C., where his competence and efficiency were fully recognised (in August 1914 he told a friend that the papers finally discharging him from the O.T.C. were marked 'Excellent' beside 'General Efficiency'). He also played football for the school, though he was not very interested in team sports. His chief athletic interest was walking and running, which he did alone, over the Downs, seeking an understanding of life through his communion with nature:

The gates are open on the road
That leads to beauty and to God.

The Downs enticed him to learn not only more of Man, but more of the timelessness of Earth. There, where men had lived and died for generations past, Charles Sorley learned a sense of proportion.

During his last year at school he began to establish himself as a poet by publishing more than a dozen poems in the *Marlburian,* and the starting point for most of these poems was the country around Marlborough. History was in the very ground beneath him and it was rich with the legacy of all the ages but the men who had made history were long dead and all but forgotten. Continuity was preserved, not in man, but in the earth and the countryside, in the trees and the winds and the formation of the Downs. But though these were the starting point for his poems they were rarely his actual subject. Like Wordsworth, Sorley built his philosophy of life upon the mystical affinity between nature and man and the majority of his poems explore this philosophy. He was constantly seeking some sort of 'Promised Land' of the imagination and he came nearest to it in the solitariness of the Downs in rain and wind. Though Wordsworth does not figure among the poets for whom Sorley expressed admiration his influence sometimes appears to be strong, as in the poem 'Marlborough':

I, who have walked along her downs in dreams,
And known her tenderness, and felt her might,
And sometimes by her meadows and her streams
Have drunk deep-storied secrets of delight,

Have had my moments there, when I have been
Unwittingly aware of something more,
Some beautiful aspect, that I had seen
With mute unspeculative eyes before;

Have had my times, when, though the earth did wear
Her self-same trees and grasses, I could see
The revelation that is always there,
But somehow is not always clear to me.

For Wordsworth, however, Man as a sentient living being was an elemental part of nature, but Sorley hardly ever wrote of living men; yet he was fascinated by the lives of the men of old, now not only part of history, but part of the ground beneath his feet. It was his deep-felt experience of history at this time that gave him his mature attitude towards war and death in 1914 and '15. In the peace and security of the pre-war years he often thought deeply on the significance of life and death, and looking back at battles long ago, from a time before Europe was under threat of war, he saw war as a testing experience, but no more so than the war against the elements, waged ceaselessly throughout history:

And here we strove, and here we felt each vein
Ice-bound, each limb fast-frozen, all night long.

And here we held communion with the rain
That lashed us into manhood with its thong,
Cleansing through pain.
And the wind visited us and made us strong.

There is clearly something of the sense of Brooke's first 1914 sonnet in Sorley's attitude here – war is seen as a cleansing, stirring force – but coupled with this is a sense of history which suggested to him the unimportance of individual man. The beliefs tentatively explored at this time were to serve him in good stead when war came.

During his time at Marlborough Sorley's future seemed to be secure. His family expected that he would move on from school to read classics at university and from thence go into the Indian Civil Service. As time went on, however, the idea appealed to him less and less. He was anxious to do some sort of social work and at one time, after a row with a young classics master, he considered leaving Marlborough and becoming an Elementary schoolteacher. In a lengthy discussion with the school music master he was persuaded that his best course would be to go to university and get a degree so that he could teach in a Working Man's College or a night-school. Once his mind was made up he wrote a long explanatory letter to his parents in January 1913 (see page 83) and from that time the idea of the Indian Civil Service was dropped. Despite his affection for Marlborough, he decided that he would like to leave school at the end of the year; it was not that school was becoming irksome, but that he enjoyed it too much; it cushioned him from life. He now set his sights on a scholarship to Oxford which he won in December 1913. This achieved, and his place in University College, Oxford, assured for the following October, it was agreed between him, his father and Dr. Wynne-Wilson, then Master of Marlborough, that he should leave Marlborough and see something of the world. Always ready to embrace new experiences, and always full of a zest for living, he travelled in January 1914 to Schwerin in Mecklenburg, where he lived in the family of Herr Doktor and Frau Bieder and took German lessons. He was very happy there and got on well with the family. Frau Bieder read German with him and took him to the theatre and opera and in general fussed and cosseted him, having no sons of her own to lavish her affection on.

He now threw himself into the life of Schwerin, joining the local Hockey Club and taking part in all the local activities. He soon came to know and love the German people and to delight in a life so different from what he had known previously. Germany had become a sort of 'Promised Land' to him: 'I have a kind of feeling that towards the end of January I left Egypt and arrived safely in Canaan' he wrote to the Master of Marlborough on the 20th of February 1914 (see page 87). It was an ironic turn of events; intensely devoted to his old school and to the English countryside, an active and proficient member of the O.T.C., he found himself suddenly experiencing ardently the emotion of patriotism, not to England or Scotland, but to the country against which, in little more than six months, he would be preparing to fight. In the letter quoted above he told how he saw two companies of German soldiers returning from field exercises singing lustily 'something glorious and senseless about the Fatherland'; he was stirred to comment,

> And when I got home, I felt I was a German, and proud to be a German: when the tempest of the singing was at its loudest, I felt that perhaps I could die for Deutschland – and I have never had an inkling of that feeling about England, and never shall.

Perhaps it was his new-won freedom which made Sorley feel so ecstatic about Germany, for during his last year at school he had begun to question the sense of bondage imposed on the life of Public Schoolboys:

> *. . .when I have a son of mine*
> *He shan't be made to droop and pine,*
> *Bound down and forced by rule and rod*
> *To serve a God who is no God*

he wrote in June 1913. Yet the only poem which we know for sure dates from this period of liberty is the nostalgic 'Marlborough'. It does not, in fact, appear to have been a very productive period creatively. Nevertheless, Sorley had decided to embark on his first novel and early in February he wrote to tell a friend that he had 'written three brilliant chapters of it'. It is unlikely that he would ever have become a novelist. His poems are concerned with philosophic thought, not with people, nor with events. His short verse drama 'The Other Wise Man', which takes its origin from the old legend of the fourth wise man, moves slowly and is concerned, not with what happens, but with the idea that God can be found in the beauty of nature, in the trees, the hills and the sky. Nothing in the work seems to justify the comment which Robert Nichols in his *Anthology of War Poetry* claims that Robert Bridges made to him, 'that, had Sorley lived he might have become our greatest dramatist since Shakespeare'. These words are quoted with apparent approval by John Press in his article on Sorley in *Review of English Literature* (VII.2: 1966) when he speculates upon what Sorley might have achieved had he survived the war. But 'The Other Wise Man' is a static verse drama, no more meant to be acted than were the contemporary verse dramas of Abercrombie and Bottomley, or those of Isaac Rosenberg. It is to be regretted that there appears to be no trace of Sorley's novel. As he makes no further reference to it we must assume that it was an abortive attempt and did not progress beyond the three brilliant chapters.

At the beginning of May Sorley left Schwerin for Jena, where he enrolled in the University for a term. For a brief period he had wanted to go to Munich, but his father preferred to send him to Jena and once the decision was made Charles accepted it cheerfully. Once there, he swam, played tennis, returned to the classics and read some Greek, progressed with his German studies and made many friends; at the University he took classes in philosophy and political economy. It was a busy, but fruitful time and one of great intellectual growth. He worshipped Goethe, discovered modern German poetry – 'Rilke and Hölderlin and sich' as he described them – and decided that Ibsen's *John Gabriel Borkman* was 'the finest thing ever written'. His youthful enthusiasm for Masefield and Housman waned, but he retained his schoolboy admiration for Richard Jefferies.

'In the midst of my setting up and smashing of deities – Masefield, Hardy, Goethe – I always fall back on Richard Jefferies wandering about in the background. I have at least the tie of locality with him', he wrote in July 1914.

He was not so engrossed in educating himself that he did not realize the peculiarly 'offensive and aggressive' character of the German corps students, but he seemed unaware of the approaching war. Whilst enmity in Europe was growing he was fostering amity. On the 24th of July 1914, the day after Austria-Hungary presented its ultimatum to Serbia, Sorley wrote to a friend telling him how he had perjured himself to save his landlady's tame squirrel from destruction, but there was no word of the growing shadow of war over Europe. Two days later a letter to his cousin made it clear that the war hysteria had begun and Sorley himself had been taken up in it, even to the point of momentarily admiring the usually despised corps student:

> It is a fine sight to see all the corps dressed up in their old-fashioned costumes, carrying torches, singing through the town at midnight. It almost makes one wish that one was an 'inkorporierter' too. Tonight, I'm afraid, they are making a war demonstration and shouting 'Down with the Serbs'. We are altogether having a thrilling time at present: with new editions of the papers coming out every hour, each time with wilder rumours.

The rumours did not disturb him unduly, however, for despite the international tension he left Jena on the 28th of July for a walking tour through the Moselle valley with a friend; that day Austria-Hungary declared war on Serbia, but Sorley, walking in the countryside was unaware of it. He intended to return to Britain on the 16th of August, but on the 2nd he and his friend were arrested as spies and put in prison. Their imprisonment lasted for only a few hours and Charles arrived back home on the 6th of August. He immediately applied for a Commission and a few days later was gazetted as a temporary second Lieutenant in the Suffolk Regiment. He was one of the first officers of Kitchener's Army. At the time he had twinges of conscience that he had not joined 'the Regulars as a Tommy', but he soon settled into his new role of officer in training. He did not realize that he had in fact placed himself in the position of the greatest danger, for the mortality among Junior Officers in France was higher than that of any other rank.

Sorley's attitude to the war was, perforce, ambivalent. In the preceding months he had grown to know and love Germany and her people and could not condemn them utterly. 'We are not fighting a bully, but a bigot', he wrote to his Marlborough friend, A.J. Hopkinson, in October, '...I regard the war as one between sisters, between Martha and Mary, the efficient and intolerant against the casual and sympathetic' (see page 94). Though he came down on the side of tolerance and sympathy he could never subscribe to the anti-German feeling which swept through Britain. Yet in the letter quoted above he does subscribe to the kind of romantic sentiment which was rife among young men from the privileged classes in the early days of the war, suggesting that through the war Germany was 'doing the world a service...by giving them something to live and die for'.

At first the Army in training was for Sorley a soul-destroying experience. His biggest complaint was against the monotony of his existence. Having spent the previous six months widening his intellectual horizons he now found himself without time to read, or even to think, unable to pursue any of his own interests. As for his poetry, he felt the utter impossibility of 'writing poetry in the Officers' Mess'. By the beginning of 1915, however, he was able to write to a friend saying, 'I have begun to read again'. He was reading D.H. Lawrence, probably *Sons and Lovers,* which had been published in 1913. He had begun to write poetry again too and after he had been disappointed of a promised leave in December 1914 he 'made up three poems and went to bed early on the strength of it'. In fact, over a dozen of his printed poems date from this period; they were sent home in batches on sheets of paper often carried about in his pocket for some time. Sending some home in a letter to his mother in April 1915 he explained that they had been written hurriedly and that he had 'had no time for the final touch nor seem likely to have for some time'.

Not many of the poems written at this time make direct reference to the war. What is perhaps most noticeable is the sense of loss, of lacking an anchor; it seems that Sorley had not come to terms with his new life; he had become a seeker again; he is concerned with journeys and wanderings, but the Promised Land is not at the end of the road. 'Le Revenant', one of his rare poems which tells a story, denies the protagonist his home-coming; 'Lost' is concerned with an uncertainty about which direction to take in life; 'To Poets' opens with the words 'We are the homeless'; the two poems inspired by Ibsen, 'Brand' and 'Peer Gynt' have the same sense of yearning: 'I wander unfulfilled: and see strange faces'. It is not surprising that Sorley suffered from longing and uncertainty at this time. When in January 1914 he had 'arrived safely in Canaan', his Canaan was Germany; now he was personally involved in war against his Canaan. Thus, from the outset, he had a wider view of the conflict than was common in the early months of the war; he was able to appreciate the excitement and the challenge, the extolling of 'bravery, endurance and the obvious forms of self-sacrifice', but he put them in their true perspective as a 'glorification of the second-best' (from a letter to A.E. Hutchinson, October 1914). At the same time he was acutely aware of the false romanticism which lauded everything English as 'good' and condemned everything German as evil:

> England – I am sick of the sound of the word. In training to fight for England, I am training to fight for that deliberate hypocrisy, that terrible middle-class sloth of outlook and appalling 'imaginative indolence' that has marked us out from generation to generation... I think that after the war all brave men will renounce their country and confess that they are strangers and pilgrims upon the earth.... But all these convictions are useless for me to state since I have not had the courage of them. What a worm one is under the cart-wheels – big clumsy

> careless lumbering cart-wheels – of public opinion. I might have been giving my mind to fight against Sloth and Stupidity: instead, I am giving my body (by a refinement of cowardice) to fight against the most enterprising nation in the world.
>
> (Letter to A.E. Hutchinson, 14 November 1914)

Sorley's few war poems of this period offer a balanced view of the war situation as he saw it, but his war so far had been the army in training. What may have been his first poem of the war, the sonnet 'To Germany', is in no way romantic except perhaps in the hope expressed in the sestet:

Grown more loving-kind and warm
We'll grasp firm hands and laugh at the old pain,
When it is peace.

Sorley perceived what few Britons perceived at that time, that there was a lack of understanding on both sides and that peace depended upon understanding. Having known and loved Germany and many of her people, he could not subscribe to the jingoistic view that all Germans were criminals; if they were blind, so were we: 'You are blind like us'. Written about the same time as 'To Germany', the much-anthologised poem, 'All the hills and vales along' has continued to puzzle readers over the years; on the whole, however, criticism has been favourable. It has generally been seen as a marching song, though its somewhat disturbed rhythm does not suggest this. Again, it has been compared with Grenfell's 'Into Battle', but John Press, in the article referred to above (page 18), suggests that it is 'a darker, more ironical poem' than Grenfell's. In his essay on Sorley in *Out of Battle* Jon Silkin accepts the irony, but feels that the 'ambiguity of the poem lies in the relation between man and nature'; he goes on to say that the poem is 'awry because it postulates a nature-man antagonism in the context of an antagonism between men, in which nature is at best incidental'. He has misunderstood Sorley's attitude towards, not nature, but the earth. For Sorley, earth was not hostile to man; it embraced him, as it had Christ, welcomed him, and only through death could man become part of earth – thus Christ was taken into earth's keeping, whilst Barabbas was rejected:

Little live, great pass.
Jesus Christ and Barabbas
Were found the same day.
This died, that went his way.

Sorley saw Man as eternized only through death:

All the music of their going...
Earth will echo still, when foot
Lies numb and voice mute.

Only through death could Man (as distinct from individual men) flourish:

Sow your gladness for earth's reaping,
So you may be glad, though sleeping.
Strew your gladness on earth's bed,
So be merry, so be dead.

It is perhaps surprising that the poem has been so popular for it embodies a philosophy difficult to comprehend. Sorley stated this philosophy quite succinctly in a letter written to a friend in November 1914: 'The earth even more than Christ is the ultimate ideal of what man should strive to be' – earth (ironically) is what man should aspire to. Such a philosophy, rooted deeply in several of his last poems, enabled Sorley, even more than Christian belief would have done, to look at death without fear. It explains too the sense of indifference and of impersonality which informs the poem 'A hundred thousand million mites we go', with its otherwise puzzling comment in the second from last line, 'Some black with death – but most are bright with Day!' It is not to Christ men are returning, but to earth, the 'ultimate ideal' of what they should aspire to.

From about March 1915 Sorley's battalion expected any

moment to go to France, but the first excitement was over before they went: 'If we had gone out earlier we would have gone out with a thrill in poetic-martial vein', he wrote to his mother at that time. It was not until the last day of May that they finally embarked for France: When they arrived Sorley's company were billetted in idyllic surroundings in northern France. 'We are in a little hamlet, or rather settlement of farms', he explained to his parents in his first letter,

> the men on straw, the officers in old four-posters: within sound of the guns. Nothing disturbs these people. I have never felt so restful. There is cidre and cidre and cidre to drink, which reminds one of Normandy. And over all hangs the smell of never-lifted manure.... So far our company are separated from the rest. It is like a picnic, and the weather is of the best.

(see page 98)

Soon after he arrived in France his parents suggested that they should have a small volume of his poems printed, but Sorley thought the proposal 'premature'. He felt that he had not had time to brood over and revise his poems, nor had he then any opportunity for selection. Thus he begged them to go no further with the proposal, commenting, 'For three years or the duration of the war, let be'. The first edition of his poems was, in fact, published posthumously a little over six months later.

For a month his battalion remained well behind the lines but in July they moved up to Support Trenches; things were still fairly quiet, but it was now that Sorley first came face to face with sudden death when, out on a bombing raid, one of his own bombers blew himself up through mishandling his grenade. He himself suffered a minor head wound, but was on duty again the next morning. He began to be inured to such happenings and on the 26th of August he wrote to Arthur Watts who had been one of his tutors at Jena, 'One is hardened by now: purged of all false pity: perhaps more selfish than before' (see page 105).

In late August he was promoted Captain; because of this promotion his leave, due in mid-September, had to be postponed, for he had to take his turn in a different queue. Thus, when the Battle of Loos began, he moved up with his Company to the Front Line. He hoped for leave towards the end of October, but by that time it was too late, for he was caught by a sniper's bullet in what was one of the most ill-conceived and mismanaged battles of the early war years.

Of the six poems which we know for certain date from his service in France, four are about death. John Press, in the article quoted above, suggests that it was during his period of army training that Sorley first 'hints at the awareness of death overshadowing him and all his companions'. However, Sorley had come to terms with death at a very early age. On the 8th of November 1910 his schoolfriend, Arthur Bethune-Baker died after a very short illness. Arthur's memory remained with Charles for the rest of his life and writing to Mrs. Bethune-Baker on the fourth anniversary of his friends's death he remarked, 'for some one else beside you he cannot ever be called dead'. Quite a number of the earlier poems have reference to the idea of death, so that death in war was simply a culmination of all Sorley's earlier thoughts on death. The conventional 'In Memoriam', written in memory of his schoolfriend, Sidney Woodroffe, who was killed in action in July 1915, was published in *The Marlburian* after Sorley's own death. It is reminiscent of Rupert Brooke's fourth sonnet, 'These hearts were woven of human joys and cares', (incidentally, the only one of the five that Sorley admired) both in its sentiment and in its vocabulary; it illustrates the fact that the belief that one's friends died heroically and gloriously was the last romantic illusion; it does not tell us anything about Sorley.

The two sonnets on death, written three months earlier, soon after he went to France, are more typical. Jon Silkin is, of course, wrong when he says in the work quoted above that by the time he was writing these he had 'experienced trench fighting'; he was still well behind the lines and though he may have felt death pointing out his road he had not seen the horrors of front line wounding and mutilation. The sonnets contain an acceptance of death untrammelled by a knowledge of the bestiality of death in war. Sorley again seemed to be in search of his Promised Land.

A homeless land and friendless, but a land
I did not know and that I wished to know.

From the second sonnet we are forced to assume that the Promised Land is reached only through man's union with earth whence his

...Promise, withered long and sped,
Is touched, stirs, rises, opens and grows sweet
And blossoms...

Sorley's last poem, sent home with his papers from France, is again a sonnet. Here we see a tightening of his sentiments – death is still accepted, but there is more awareness of its nature in war: 'mouthless dead...gashed head...blind eyes' suggest not only the horror of death in battle, but also the finality of death. Coupled with this is a noticeable harshness towards any sentimentality on the part of the living; the comfort of mourning is denied to the bereaved, as is also the comfort of reflected glory:

Give them not praise....
Nor honour. It is easy to be dead.

It was a bitter poem to arrive home after his own death.

Dying at the age of twenty, Sorley had no chance to develop his poetic powers; his greatness remains in potential, rather than in fulfilment. Few, if any, of his poems are perfect; in most of them the thought outstrips the technique. Sorley was technically rather conventional. A good number of his poems are in four-line stanzas; his favourite rhyme-scheme was ABAB; he had a good ear for rhyme, but rhythmically was less certain, yet the rhythmic irregularities of some of his later poems seem to give them greater strength. His choice of words, too, is often weak, disturbing a carefully built up train of thought with an incongrous idea. Yet we must remember that he was not given time to polish and perfect. Nevertheless, his ideas are always interesting and never more so than when he was writing of war and death, and among his small output is at least a handful of fine poems. Of immense interest too are the numerous letters he wrote to his family and friends, lively well-written prose, suggesting perhaps a gift that he did not have a chance to develop. The letters are especially valuable in giving a picture of a gifted young man developing from boyhood to rapid maturity. They are essential reading to anyone interested in the literature of the Great War.

Hilda D. Spear
Dundee University
February 1978

TEXTUAL NOTE

The text for the poems in this edition is taken mainly from the fifth edition of *Marlborough and Other Poems,* published by Cambridge University Press in 1922. The first edition was published in 1916. The fourth edition, published in 1919, was intended by Sorley's father to be the definitive edition of the poems and it was re-arranged and re-set. Of this, the fifth edition was an exact reprint, except for one or two minor alterations made from manuscripts.

The present edition re-arranges the poems in chronological order as far as possible. It varies from the fifth edition of *Marlborough and Other Poems* in the text of 'To J.B.' (p. 73). This poem was originally published without title and printed from a transcript made by 'J.B.', from which he omitted a number of lines which he felt were too flattering to him. The poem as it is now printed is taken from a photocopy of the original manuscript and contains not only the missing lines, but also a number of minor corrections (see note on the poem).

The text for the letters is taken from *The Letters of Charles Sorley,* published by Cambridge University Press in 1919.

POEMS
1912 - 1915

RAIN

When the rain is coming down,
And all Court is still and bare,
And the leaves fall wrinkled, brown,
Through the kindly winter air,
And in tattered flannels I
'Sweat' beneath a tearful sky,
And the sky is dim and grey,
And the rain is coming down,
And I wander far away
From the little red-capped town:
There is something in the rain
That would bid me to remain:
There is something in the wind
That would whisper, 'Leave behind
All this land of time and rules,
Land of bells and early schools.
Latin, Greek and College food
Do you precious little good.
Leave them: if you would be free
Follow, follow, after me!'

When I reach 'Four Miler's height,
And I look abroad again
On the skies of dirty white
And the drifting veil of rain,
And the bunch of scattered hedge
Dimly swaying on the edge,
And the endless stretch of downs
Clad in green and silver gowns;
There is something in their dress
Of bleak barren ugliness,
That would whisper, 'You have read
Of a land of light and glory:
But believe not what is said.
'Tis a kingdom bleak and hoary,

Where the winds and tempests call
And the rain sweeps over all.
Heed not what the preachers say
Of a good land far away.
Here's a better land and kind
And it is not far to find.'

Therefore, when we rise and sing
Of a distant land, so fine,
Where the bells for ever ring,
And the suns for ever shine:
Singing loud and singing grand,
Of a happy far-off land,
O! I smile to hear the song,
For I know that they are wrong,
That the happy land and gay
Is not very far away,
And that I can get there soon
Any rainy afternoon.

And when summer comes again,
And the downs are dimpling green,
And the air is free from rain,
And the clouds no longer seen:
Then I know that they have gone
To find a new camp further on,
Where there is no shining sun
To throw light on what is done,
Where the summer can't intrude
On the fort where winter stood:
—Only blown and drenching grasses,
Only rain that never passes,
Moving mists and sweeping wind,
And I follow them behind!

October 1912

A CALL TO ACTION

I

A thousand years have passed away,
 Cast back your glances on the scene,
Compare this England of to-day
 With England as she once has been.

Fast beat the pulse of living then:
 The hum of movement, throb of war
The rushing mighty sound of men
 Reverberated loud and far.

They girt their loins up and they trod
 The path of danger, rough and high;
For Action, Action was their god,
 'Be up and doing' was their cry.

A thousand years have passed away;
 The sands of life are running low;
The world is sleeping out her day;
 The day is dying—be it so.

A thousand years have passed amain;
 The sands of life are running thin;
Thought is our leader—Thought is vain;
 Speech is our goddess—Speech is sin.

II

It needs no thought to understand,
 No speech to tell, nor sight to see
That there has come upon our land
 The curse of Inactivity.

We do not see the vital point
  That 'tis the eighth, most deadly, sin
To wail, 'The world is out of joint'—
  And not attempt to put it in.

We see the swollen stream of crime
  Flow hourly past us, thick and wide;
We gaze with interest for a time,
  And pass by on the other side.

We see the tide of human sin
  Rush roaring past our very door,
And scarcely one man plunges in
  To drag the drowning to the shore.

We, dull and dreamy, stand and blink,
  Forgetting glory, strength and pride,
Half—listless watchers on the brink,
  Half—ruined victims of the tide.

III

We question, answer, make defence,
  We sneer, we scoff, we criticize,
We wail and moan our decadence,
  Enquire, investigate, surmise;

We preach and prattle, peer and pry
  And fit together two and two:
We ponder, argue, shout, swear, lie—
  We will not, for we cannot, DO.

Pale puny soldiers of the pen,
  Absorbed in this your inky strife,
Act as of old, when men were men,
  England herself and life yet life.

October 1912

A TALE OF TWO CAREERS

I SUCCESS

He does not dress as other men,
 His 'kish' is loud and gay,
His 'side' is as the 'side' of ten
 Because his 'barnes' are grey.

His head has swollen to a size
 Beyond the proper size for heads,
He metaphorically buys
 The ground on which he treads.

Before his face of haughty grace
 The ordinary mortal cowers:
A 'forty-cap' has put the chap
 Into another world from ours.

The funny little world that lies
 'Twixt High Street and the Mound
Is just a swarm of buzzing flies
 That aimlessly go round:

If one is stronger in the limb
 Or better able to work hard,
It's quite amusing to watch him
 Ascending heavenward.

But if one cannot work or play
 (Who loves the better part too well),
It's really sad to see the lad
 Retained compulsorily in hell.

II FAILURE

We are the wasters, who have no
  Hope in this world here, neither fame,
Because we cannot collar low
  Nor write a strange dead tongue the same
  As strange dead men did long ago.

We are the weary, who begin
  The race with joy, but early fail,
Because we do not care to win
  A race that goes not to the frail
And humble: only the proud come in.

We are the shadow-forms, who pass
  Unheeded hence from work and play.
We are to-day, but like the grass
  That to-day is, we pass away;
And no one stops to say 'Alas!'

Though we have little, all we have
  We give our School. And no return
We can expect for what we gave;
  No joys; only a summons stern,
'Depart, for others entrance crave!'

As soon as she can clearly prove
  That from us is no hope of gain,
Because we only bring her love
  And cannot bring her strength or brain,
She tells us, 'Go: it is enough.'

She turns us out at seventeen,
  We may not know her any more,
And all our life with her has been
  A life of seeing others score,
While we sink lower and are mean.

We have seen others reap success
Full-measure. None has come to us.
Our life has been one failure. Yes,
But does not God prefer it thus?
God does not also praise success.

And for each failure that we meet,
And for each place we drop behind,
Each toil that holds our aching feet,
Each star we seek and never find,
God, knowing, gives us comfort meet,

The School we care for has not cared
To cherish nor keep our names to be
Memorials. God hath prepared
Some better thing for us, for we
His hopes have known, His failures shared.

November 1912

PEACE

There is silence in the evening when the long days cease,
And a million men are praying for an ultimate release
From strife and sweat and sorrow—they are praying for peace.
But God is marching on.

Peace for a people that is striving to be free!
Peace for the children of the wild wet sea!
Peace for the seekers of the promised land—do we
Want peace when God has none?

We pray for rest and beauty that we know we
cannot earn,
And ever are we asking for a honey-sweet return;
But God will make it bitter, make it bitter, till we
learn
That with tears the race is run.

And did not Jesus perish to bring men, not peace,
But a sword, a sword for battle and a sword that
should not cease?
Two thousand years have passed us. Do we still
want peace
Where the sword of Christ has shone?

Yes, Christ perished to present us with a sword,
That strife should be our portion and more strife
our reward,
For toil and tribulation and the glory of the Lord
And the sword of Christ are one.

If you want to know the beauty of the thing called
rest,
Go, get it from the poets, who will tell you it is best
(And their words are sweet as honey) to lie flat upon
your chest
And sleep till life is gone.

I know that there is beauty where the low streams
run,
And the weeping of the willows and the big sunk
sun,
But I know my work is doing and it never shall be
done,
Though I march for ages on.

Wild is the tumult of the long grey street,
O, is it never silent from the tramping of their feet?
Here, Jesus, is Thy triumph, and here the world's
  defeat,
    For from here all peace has gone.

There's a stranger thing than beauty in the ceaseless
  city's breast,
In the throbbing of its fever—and the wind is in the
  west,
And the rain is driving forward where there is no
  rest,
    For the Lord is marching on.

December 1912

THE RIVER

He watched the river running black
  Beneath the blacker sky;
It did not pause upon its track
  Of silent instancy;
It did not hasten, nor was slack,
  But still went gliding by.

It was so black. There was no wind
  Its patience to defy.
It was not that the man had sinned,
  Or that he wished to die.
Only the wide and silent tide
  Went slowly sweeping by.

The mass of blackness moving down
 Filled full of dreams the eye;
The lights of all the lighted town
 Upon its breast did lie;
The tall black trees were upside down
 In the river phantasy.

He had an envy for its black
 Inscrutability;
He felt impatiently the lack
 Of that great law whereby
The river never travels back
 But still goes gliding by;

But still goes gliding by, nor clings
 To passing things that die,
Nor shows the secrets that it brings
 From its strange source on high.
And he felt 'We are two living things
 And the weaker one is I.'

He saw the town, that living stack
 Piled up against the sky.
He saw the river running black
 On, on and on: O, why
Could he not move along his track
 With such consistency?

He had a yearning for the strength
 That comes of unity:
The union of one soul at length
 With its twin-soul to lie:
To be a part of one great strength
 That moves and cannot die.
 * * * * * * *

He watched the river running black
  Beneath the blacker sky.
He pulled his coat about his back,
  He did not strive nor cry.
He put his foot upon the track
  That still went gliding by.

The thing that never travels back
  Received him silently.
And there was left no shred, no wrack
  To show the reason why:
Only the river running black
  Beneath the blacker sky.

February 1913

THE SEEKERS

The gates are open on the road
That leads to beauty and to God.

Perhaps the gates are not so fair,
Nor quite so bright as once they were,
When God Himself on earth did stand
And gave to Abraham His hand
And led him to a better land.

For lo! the unclean walk therein,
And those that have been soiled with sin.
The publican and harlot pass
Along: they do not stain its grass.
In it the needy has his share,
In it the foolish do not err.
Yes, spurned and fool and sinner stray
Along the highway and the way.

And what if all its ways are trod
By those whom sin brings near to God?
This journey soon will make them clean:
Their faith is greater than their sin.

For still they travel slowly by
Beneath the promise of the sky,
Scorned and rejected utterly;
Unhonoured; things of little worth
Upon the highroads of this earth;
Afflicted, destitute and weak:
Nor find the beauty that they seek,
The God they set their trust upon:
—Yet still they march rejoicing on.

March 1913

BARBURY CAMP

We burrowed night and day with tools of lead,
Heaped the bank up and cast it in a ring
And hurled the earth above. And Caesar said,
'Why, it is excellent. I like the thing.'
We, who are dead,
Made it, and wrought, and Caesar liked the thing.

And here we strove, and here we felt each vein
Ice-bound, each limb fast-frozen, all night long.
And here we held communion with the rain
That lashed us into manhood with its thong,
Cleansing through pain.
And the wind visited us and made us strong.

Up from around us, numbers without name,
Strong men and naked, vast, on either hand
Pressing us in, they came. And the wind came
And bitter rain, turning grey all the land.
That was our game,
To fight with men and storms, and it was grand.

For many days we fought them, and our sweat
Watered the grass, making it spring up green,
Blooming for us. And, if the wind was wet,
Our blood wetted the wind, making it keen
With the hatred
And wrath and courage that our blood had been.

So, fighting men and winds and tempests, hot
With joy and hate and battle-lust, we fell
Where we fought. And God said, 'Killed at last
then? What!
Ye that are too strong for heaven, too clean for hell,
(God said) stir not.
This be your heaven, or, if ye will, your hell.'

So again we fight and wrestle, and again
Hurl the earth up and cast it in a ring.
But when the wind comes up, driving the rain
(Each rain-drop a fiery steed), and mists rolling
Up from the plain,
This wild procession, this impetuous thing,

Hold us amazed. We mount the wind-cars, then
Whip up the steeds and drive through all the world,
Searching to find somewhere some brethren,
Sons of the winds and waters of the world.
We, who were men,
Have sought, and found no men in all this world.

Wind, that has blown here always ceaselessly,
Bringing, if any man can understand,
Might to the mighty, freedom to the free;
Wind, that has caught us, cleansed us, made us
grand,
Wind that is we
(We that were men)—make men in all this land,

That so may live and wrestle and hate that when
They fall at last exultant, as we fell,
And come to God, God may say, 'Do you come then
Mildly enquiring, is it heaven or hell?
Why! Ye were men!
Back to your winds and rains. Be these your heaven
and hell!'

24 March 1913

ROOKS

There, where the rusty iron lies,
The rooks are cawing all the day.
Perhaps no man, until he dies,
Will understand them, what they say.

The evening makes the sky like clay.
  The slow wind waits for night to rise.
The world is half-content. But they

Still trouble all the trees with cries,
  That know, and cannot put away,
The yearning to the soul that flies
  From day to night, from night to day.

21 June 1913

WHAT YOU WILL

O come and see, it's such a sight,
So many boys all doing right:
To see them underneath the yoke,
Blindfolded by the elder folk,
Move at a most impressive rate
Along the way that is called straight.
O, it is comforting to know
They're in the way they ought to go.
But don't you think it's far more gay
To see them slowly leave the way
And limp and loose themselves and fall?
O, that's the nicest thing of all.
I love to see this sight, for then
I know they are becoming men,
And they are tiring of the shrine
Where things are really not divine.

I do not know if it seems brave
The youthful spirit to enslave,
And hedge about, lest it should grow.
I don't know if it's better so
In the long end. I only know
That when I have a son of mine,
He shan't be made to droop and pine,
Bound down and forced by rule and rod

To serve a God who is no God.
But I'll put custom on the shelf
And make him find his God himself,
Perhaps he'll find him in a tree,
Some hollow trunk, where you can see.
Perhaps the daisies in the sod
Will open out and show him God.
Or will he meet him in the roar
Of breakers as they beat the shore?
Or in the spiky stars that shine?
Or in the rain (where I found mine)?
Or in the city's giant moan?
  —A God who will be all his own,
  To whom he can address a prayer
  And love him, for he is so fair,
  And see with eyes that are not dim
  And build a temple meet for him.

30 June 1913

STONES

This field is almost white with stones
  That cumber all its thirsty crust.
And underneath, I know, are bones,
  And all around is death and dust.

And if you love a livelier hue—
  O, if you love the youth of year,
When all is clean and green and new,
  Depart. There is no summer here.

Albeit, to me there lingers yet
  In this forbidding stony dress
The impotent and dim regret
  For some forgotten restlessness.

Dumb, imperceptibly astir,
  These relics of an ancient race,
These men, in whom the dead bones were
  Still fortifying their resting-place.

Their field of life was white with stones;
  Good fruit to earth they never brought.
O, in these bleached and buried bones
  Was neither love nor faith nor thought.

But like the wind in this bleak place,
  Bitter and bleak and sharp they grew,
And bitterly they ran their race,
  A brutal, bad, unkindly crew:

Souls like the dry earth, hearts like stone,
  Brains like that barren bramble-tree:
Stern, sterile, senseless, mute, unknown–
  But bold, O, bolder far than we!

14 July 1913

EAST KENNET CHURCH AT EVENING

I stood amongst the corn, and watched
  The evening coming down.
The rising vale was like a queen,
  And the dim church her crown.

Crown-like it stood against the hills.
  Its form was passing fair.
I almost saw the tribes go up
  To offer incense there.

And far below the long vale stretched.
  As a sleeper she did seem
That after some brief restlessness
  Has now begun to dream.

(All day the wakefulness of men,
  Their lives and labours brief,
Have broken her long troubled sleep.
  Now, evening brings relief.)

There was no motion there, nor sound.
  She did not seem to rise.
Yet was she wrapping herself in
  Her grey of night-disguise.

For now no church nor tree nor fold
  Was visible to me:
Only that fading into one
  Which God must sometimes see.

No coloured glory streaked the sky
  To mark the sinking sun.
There was no redness in the west
  To tell that day was done.

Only, the greyness of the eve
  Grew fuller than before.
And, in its fulness, it made one
  Of what had once been more.

There was much beauty in that sight
  That man must not long see.
God dropped the kindly veil of night
  Between its end and me.

24 July 1913

ROOKS (II)

There is such cry in all these birds,
  More than can ever be express'd;
If I should put it into words,
  You would agree it were not best
  To wake such wonder from its rest.

But since to-night the world is still
  And only they and I astir,
We are united, will to will,
  By bondage tighter, tenderer
  Than any lovers ever were.

And if, of too much labouring,
  All that I see around should die
(There is such sleep in each green thing,
  Such weariness in all the sky),
  We would live on, these birds and I.

Yet how? since everything must pass
  At evening with the sinking sun,
And Christ is gone, and Barabbas,
  Judas and Jesus, gone, clean gone,
  Then how shall I live on?

Yet surely Judas must have heard
  Amidst his torments the long cry
Of some lone Israelitish bird,
  And on it, ere he came to die,
  Thrown all his spirit's agony.

And that immortal cry which welled
  For Judas, ever afterwards
Passion on passion still has swelled
  And sweetened: so to-night these birds
  Will take my words, will take my words,

And wrapping them in music meet
  Will sing their spirit through the sky,
Strange and unsatisfied and sweet:
  That, when stock-dead am I, am I,
  O, that can never die!

25 July 1913

AUTUMN DAWN

And this is morning. Would you think
That this was the morning, when the land
Is full of heavy eyes that blink
Half-opened, and the tall trees stand
Too tired to shake away the drops
Of passing night that cling around
Their branches and weigh down their tops:
And the grey sky leans on the ground?
The thrush sings once or twice, but stops
Affrighted by the silent sound.
The sheep, scarce moving, munches, moans.
The slow herd mumbles, thick with phlegm.
The grey road-mender, hacking stones,
Is now become as one of them.
Old mother Earth has rubbed her eyes
And stayed, so senseless, lying down.
Old mother is too tired to rise
And lay aside her grey nightgown,
And come with singing and with strength
In loud exuberance of day,
Swift-darting. She is tired at length,
Done up, past bearing, you would say.
She'll come no more in lust of strife,
In hedge's leap, and wild bird's cries,
In winds that cut you like a knife,
In days of laughter and swift skies,
That palpably pulsate with life,
With life that kills, with life that dies.
But in a morning such as this
Is neither life nor death to see,
Only that state which some call bliss,
Grey hopeless immortality.
Earth is at length bedrid. She is
Supinest of the things that be:
And stilly, heavy with long years,

Brings forth such days in dumb regret,
Immortal days, that rise in tears,
And cannot, though they strive to, set.
* * * * * *
The mists do move. The wind takes breath.
The sun appeareth over there,
And with red fingers hasteneth
From Earth's grey bed the clothes to tear.
And strike the heavy mist's dank tent.
And Earth uprises with a sigh.
She is astir. She is not spent.
And yet she lives and yet can die.
The grey road-mender from the ditch
Looks up. He has not looked before.
The stunted tree sways like the witch
It was: 'tis living witch once more.
The winds are washen. In the deep
Dew of the morn they've washed. The skies
Are changing dress. The clumsy sheep
Bound, and earth's many bosoms rise,
And earth's green tresses spring and leap
About her brow. The earth has eyes,
The earth has voice, the earth has breath,
As o'er the land and through the air,
With wingéd sandals, Life and Death
Speed hand in hand—that winsome pair!

16 September 1913

RETURN

Still stand the downs so wise and wide?
Still shake the trees their tresses grey?
I thought their beauty might have died
Since I had been away.

I might have known the things I love,
The winds, the flocking birds' full cry,
The trees that toss, the downs that move,
Were longer things than I.

Lo, earth that bows before the wind,
  With wild green children overgrown,
And all her bosoms, many-whinned,
  Receive me as their own.

The birds are hushed and fled: the cows
  Have ceased at last to make long moan,
They only think to browse and browse
  Until the night is grown.

The wind is stiller than it was,
  And dumbness holds the closing day.
The earth says not a word, because
  It has no word to say.

The dear soft grasses under foot
  Are silent to the listening ear.
Yet beauty never can be mute,
  And some will always hear.

18 September 1913

RICHARD JEFFERIES
(LIDDINGTON CASTLE)

I see the vision of the Vale
  Rise teeming to the rampart Down,
The fields and, far below, the pale
  Red-roofédness of Swindon town.

But though I see all things remote,
  I cannot see them with the eyes
With which ere now the man from Coate
  Looked down and wondered and was wise.

He knew the healing balm of night,
  The strong and sweeping joy of day,
The sensible and dear delight
  Of life, the pity of decay.

And many wondrous words he wrote,
  And something good to man he showed,
About the entering in of Coate,
  There, on the dusty Swindon road.

19 September 1913

J. B.

There's still a horse on Granham hill,
And still the Kennet moves, and still
Four Miler sways and is not still.
  But where is her interpreter?

The downs are blown into dismay,
The stunted trees seem all astray,
Looking for someone clad in grey
  And carrying a golf-club thing;

Who, them when he had lived among,
Gave them what they desired, a tongue.
Their words he gave them to be sung
  Perhaps were few, but they were true.

The trees, the downs, on either hand,
Still stand, as he said they would stand.
But look, the rain in all the land
  Makes all things dim with tears of him.

And recently the Kennet croons,
And winds are playing widowed tunes.
—He has not left our 'toun o' touns,'
  But taken it away with him!

October 1913

THE OTHER WISE MAN

(SCENE: *A valley with a wood on one side and a road running up to a distant hill: as it might be, the valley to the east of West Woods, that runs up to Oare Hill, only much larger.* TIME: *Autumn. Four wise men are marching hillward along the road.*)

ONE WISE MAN

I wonder where the valley ends?
On, comrades, on.

ANOTHER WISE MAN

The rain-red road,
Still shining sinuously, bends
Leagues upwards.

A THIRD WISE MAN

To the hill, O friends,
To seek the star that once has glowed
Before us; turning not to right
Nor left, nor backward once looking.
Till we have clomb—and with the night
We see the King.

ALL THE WISE MEN

The King! The King!

THE THIRD WISE MAN

Long is the road but—

A FOURTH WISE MAN

Brother, see,
There, to the left, a very aisle
Composed of every sort of tree—

THE FIRST WISE MAN

Still onward—

THE FOURTH WISE MAN

Oak and beech and birch,
Like a church, but homelier than church,
The black trunks for its walls of tile;
Its roof, old leaves; its floor, beech nuts;
The squirrels its congregation—

THE SECOND WISE MAN

Tuts!
For still we journey—

THE FOURTH WISE MAN

But the sun weaves
A water-web across the grass,
Binding their tops. You must not pass
The water cobweb.

THE THIRD WISE MAN

Hush! I say.
Onward and upward till the day—

THE FOURTH WISE MAN

Brother, that tree has crimson leaves.
You'll never see its like again.
Don't miss it. Look, it's bright with rain—

THE FIRST WISE MAN

O prating tongue. On, on.

THE FOURTH WISE MAN

And there
A toad-stool, nay, a goblin stool.
No toad sat on a thing so fair.
Wait, while I pluck—and there's—and here's
A whole ring...what?...berries?
(The Fourth Wise Man drops behind, botanizing.)

THE WISEST OF THE REMAINING THREE
WISE MEN

O fool!
Fool, fallen in this vale of tears.
His hand had touched the plough: his eyes
Looked back: no more with us, his peers,
He'll climb the hill and front the skies
And see the Star, the King, the Prize.
But we, the seekers, we who see
Beyond the mists of transiency—
Our feet down in the valley still
Are set, our eyes are on the hill.
Last night the star of God has shone,
And so we journey, up and on,
With courage clad, with swiftness shod,
All thoughts of earth behind us cast,
Until we see the lights of God,
—And what will be the crown at last?

ALL THREE WISE MEN

On, on.

(They pass on: it is already evening when the Other Wise Man limps along the road, still botanizing.)

THE OTHER WISE MAN

A vale of tears, they said!
A valley made of woes and fears,
To be passed by with muffled head
Quickly. I have not seen the tears,
Unless they take the rain for tears,
And certainly the place is wet.
Rain-laden leaves are ever licking
Your cheeks and hands...I can't get on.
There's a toad-stool that wants picking.
There, just there, a little up,
What strange things to look upon
With pink hood and orange cup!

And there are acorns, yellow–green...
They said the King was at the end.
They must have been
Wrong. For here, here, I intend
To search for him, for surely here
Are all the wares of the old year,
And all the beauty and bright prize,
And all God's colours meetly showed,
Green for the grass, blue for the skies,
Red for the rain upon the road;
And anything you like for trees,
But chiefly yellow, brown and gold,
Because the year is growing old
And loves to paint her children these.
I tried to follow...but, what do you think?
The mushrooms here are pink!
And there's old clover with black polls,
Black-headed clover, black as coals,
And toad-stools, sleek as ink!
And there are such heaps of little turns
Off the road, wet with old rain:
Each little vegetable lane
Of moss and old decaying ferns,
Beautiful in decay,
Snatching a beauty from whatever may
Be their lot, dark-red and luscious: till there pass'd
Over the many-coloured earth a grey
Film. It was evening coming down at last.
And all things hid their faces, covering up
Their peak or hood or bonnet or bright cup
In greyness, and the beauty faded fast,
With all the many-coloured coat of day.
Then I looked up, and lo! the sunset sky
Had taken the beauty from the autumn earth.
Such colour, O such colour, could not die.
The trees stood black against such revelry
Of lemon-gold and purple and crimson dye.
And even as the trees, so I

Stood still and worshipped, though by evening's
birth
I should have capped the hills and seen the King
The King? The King?
I must be miles away from my journey's end;
The others must be now nearing
The summit, glad. By now they wend
Their way far, far, ahead, no doubt.
I wonder if they've reached the end.
If they have, I have not heard them shout.

1 December 1913

MARLBOROUGH

I

Crouched where the open upland billows down
Into the valley where the river flows,
She is as any other country town,
That little lives or marks or hears or knows.

And she can teach but little. She has not
The wonder and the surging and the roar
Of striving cities. Only things forgot
That once were beautiful, but now no more,

Has she to give us. Yet to one or two
She first brought knowledge, and it was for her
To open first our eyes, until we knew
How great, immeasurably great, we were.

I, who have walked along her downs in dreams,
And known her tenderness, and felt her might,
And sometimes by her meadows and her streams
Have drunk deep-storied secrets of delight,

Have had my moments there, when I have been
Unwittingly aware of something more,

Some beautiful aspect, that I had seen
  With mute unspeculative eyes before;

Have had my times, when though the earth did wear
  Her self-same trees and grasses, I could see
The revelation that is always there,
  But somehow is not always clear to me.

II

So, long ago, one halted on his way
  And sent his company and cattle on;
His caravans trooped darkling far away
  Into the night, and he was left alone.

And he was left alone. And, lo, a man
  There wrestled with him till the break of day.
The brook was silent and the night was wan.
  And when the dawn was come, he passed away.

The sinew of the hollow of his thigh
  Was shrunken, as he wrestled there alone.
The brook was silent, but the dawn was nigh.
  The stranger named him Israel and was gone.

And the sun rose on Jacob; and he knew
  That he was no more Jacob, but had grown
A more immortal vaster spirit, who
  Had seen God face to face, and still lived on.

The plain that seemed to stretch away to God,
  The brook that saw and heard and knew no fear,
Were now the self-same soul as he who stood
  And waited for his brother to draw near.

For God had wrestled with him, and was gone.
  He looked around, and only God remained.
The dawn, the desert, he and God were one.
  —And Esau came to meet him, travel-stained.

III

So, there, when sunset made the downs look new
  And earth gave up her colours to the sky,
And far away the little city grew
  Half into sight, new-visioned was my eye.

I, who have lived, and trod her lovely earth,
  Raced with her winds and listened to her birds,
Have cared but little for their worldly worth
  Nor sought to put my passion into words.

But now it's different; and I have no rest
  Because my hand must search, dissect and spell
The beauty that is better not expressed,
  The thing that all can feel, but none can tell.

1 March 1914

THE SONG OF THE UNGIRT RUNNERS

We swing ungirded hips,
And lightened are our eyes,
The rain is on our lips,
We do not run for prize.
We know not whom we trust
Nor whitherward we fare,
But we run because we must
  Through the great wide air.

The waters of the seas
Are troubled as by storm.
The tempest strips the trees
And does not leave them warm.
Does the tearing tempest pause?
Do the tree-tops ask it why?
So we run without a cause
  'Neath the big bare sky.

The rain is on our lips,
We do not run for prize.
But the storm the water whips
And the wave howls to the skies.
The winds arise and strike it
And scatter it like sand,
And we run because we like it
Through the broad bright land.

GERMAN RAIN

The heat came down and sapped away my powers.
The laden heat came down and drowsed my brain,
Till through the weight of overcoming hours
I felt the rain.

Then suddenly I saw what more to see
I never thought: old things renewed, retrieved.
The rain that fell in England fell on me,
And I believed.

TO POETS

We are the homeless, even as you,
Who hope and never can begin.
Our hearts are wounded through and through
Like yours, but our hearts bleed within.
We too make music, but our tones
'Scape not the barrier of our bones.

We have no comeliness like you.
We toil, unlovely, and we spin.
We start, return: we wind, undo:
We hope, we err, we strive, we sin,
We love: your love's not greater, but
The lips of our loves might stay shut.

We have the evil spirits too
That shake our soul with battle-din.
But we have an eviller spirit than you,
We have a dumb spirit within:
The exceeding bitter agony
But not the exceeding bitter cry.

September 1914

WHOM THEREFORE WE IGNORANTLY WORSHIP

These things are silent. Though it may be told
Of luminous deeds that lighten land and sea,
Strong sounding actions with broad minstrelsy
Of praise, strange hazards and adventures bold,
We hold to the old things that grow not old:
Blind, patient, hungry, hopeless (without fee
Of all our hunger and unhope are we),
To the first ultimate instinct, to God we hold.

They flicker, glitter, flicker. But we bide,
We, the blind weavers of an intense fate,
Asking but this—that we may be denied:
Desiring only desire insatiate,
Unheard, unnamed, unnoticed, crucified
To our unutterable faith, we wait.

September 1914

'A HUNDRED THOUSAND MILLION MITES WE GO'

A hundred thousand million mites we go
Wheeling and tacking o'er the eternal plain,
Some black with death—and some are white with
woe.
Who sent us forth? Who takes us home again?

And there is sound of hymns of praise—to whom?
And curses—on whom curses?—snap the air.
And there is hope goes hand in hand with gloom,
And blood and indignation and despair.

And there is murmuring of the multitude
And blindness and great blindness, until some
Step forth and challenge blind Vicissitude
Who tramples on them: so that fewer come.

And nations, ankle-deep in love or hate,
Throw darts or kisses all the unwitting hour
Beside the ominous unseen tide of fate;
And there is emptiness and drink and power.

And some are mounted on swift steeds of thought
And some drag sluggish feet of stable toil.
Yet all, as though they furiously sought,
Twist turn and tussle, close and cling and coil.

A hundred thousand million mites we sway
Writhing and tossing on the eternal plain,
Some black with death—but most are bright with
  Day!
Who sent us forth? Who brings us home again?

September 1914

LOST

Across my past imaginings
  Has dropped a blindness silent and slow.
My eye is bent on other things
  Than those it once did see and know.

I may not think on those dear lands
  (O far away and long ago!)
Where the old battered signpost stands
  And silently the four roads go

East, west, south and north,
  And the cold winter winds do blow.
And what the evening will bring forth
  Is not for me nor you to know.

December 1914

BRAND

Thou trod'st the shifting sand path where man's
  race is.
The print of thy soft sandals is still clear.
I too have trodden it those prints a-near,
But the sea washes out my tired foot-traces.
And all that thou hast healed and holpen here
I yearned to heal and help and wipe the tear
Away. But still I trod unpeopled spaces.
I had no twelve to follow my pure paces.
For I had thy misgivings and thy fear,
Thy crown of scorn, thy suffering's sharp spear,
Thy hopes, thy longings—only not thy dear
Love (for my crying love would no man hear),
Thy will to love, but not thy love's sweet graces,
That deep firm foothold which no sea erases.
I think that thou wast I in bygone places
In an intense eliminated year.
Now born again in days that are more drear
I wander unfulfilled: and see strange faces.

PEER GYNT

When he was young and beautiful and bold
We hated him, for he was very strong.
But when he came back home again, quite old,
And wounded too, we could not hate him long.

For kingliness and conquest pranced he forth
Like some high-stepping charger bright with foam.
And south he strode and east and west and north
With need of crown and never need of home.

Enraged we heard high tidings of his strength
And cursed his long forgetfulness. We swore
That should he come back home some eve at length,
We would deny him, we would bar the door!

And then he came. The sound of those tired feet!
And all our home and all our hearts are his,
Where bitterness, grown weary, turns to sweet,
And envy, purged by longing, pity is.

And pillows rest beneath the withering cheek,
And hands are laid the battered brows above,
And he whom we had hated, waxen weak,
First in his weakness learns a little love.

'IF I HAVE SUFFERED PAIN'

If I have suffered pain
It is because I would.
I willed it. 'Tis no good
To murmur or complain.
I have not served the law
That keeps the earth so fair
And gives her clothes to wear,
Raiment of joy and awe.

For all, that bow to bless
That law, shall sure abide.
But man shall not abide,
And hence his gloriousness,
Lo, evening earth doth lie
All-beauteous and all peace.
Man only does not cease
From striving and from cry.

Sun sets in peace: and soon
The moon will shower her peace.
O law-abiding moon,
You hold your peace in fee!
Man, leastways, will not be
Down-bounden to these laws.
Man's spirit sees no cause
To serve such laws as these.

There yet are many seas
For man to wander in.
He yet must find out sin,
If aught of pleasance there
Remain for him to store,
His rovings to increase,
In quest of many a shore
Forbidden still to fare.

Peace sleeps the earth upon,
And sweet peace on the hill.
The waves that whimper still
At their long law-serving
(O flowing sad complaint!)
Come on and are back drawn.
Man only owns no king,
Man only is not faint.

You see, the earth is bound.
You see, the man is free.
For glorious liberty
He suffers and would die.
Grudge not then suffering
Or chastisemental cry.
O let his pain abound,
Earth's truant and earth's king!

DEUS LOQUITUR

That's what I am: a thing of no desire,
With no path to discover and no plea
To offer up, so be my altar fire
May burn before the hearth continuously,
To be
For wayward men a steadfast light to see.

They know me in the morning of their days,
But ere noontide forsake me, to discern
New lore and hear new riddles. But moonrays
Bring them back footsore, humble, bent, a-burn
To turn
And warm them by my fire which they did spurn.

They flock together like tired birds. 'We sought
Full many stars in many skies to see,
But ever knowledge disappointment brought.
Thy light alone, Lord, burneth steadfastly.'
Ah me!
Then it is I who fain would wayward be.

LE REVENANT

He trod the oft-remembered lane
(Now smaller-seeming than before
When first he left his father's door
For newer things), but still quite plain

(Though half-benighted now) upstood
Old landmarks, ghosts across the lane
That brought the Bygone back again:
Shorn haystacks and the rooky wood;

The guide post, too, which once he clomb
  To read the figures: fourteen miles
  To Swindon, four to Clinton Stiles,
And only half a mile to home:

And far away the one homestead, where—
  Behind the day now not quite set
  So that he saw in silhouette
Its chimneys still stand black and bare—

He noticed that the trees were not
  So big as when he journeyed last
  That way. For greatly now he passed
Striding above the hedges, hot

With hopings, as he passed by where
  A lamp before him glanced and stayed
  Across his path, so that his shade
Seemed like a giant's moving there.

The dullness of the sunken sun
  He marked not, nor how dark it grew,
  Nor that strange flapping bird that flew
Above: he thought but of the One....

He topped the crest and crossed the fence,
  Noticed the garden that it grew
  As erst, noticed the hen-house too
(The kennel had been altered since).

It seemed so unchanged and so still.
  (Could it but be the past arisen
  For one short night from out of prison?)
He reached the big-bowed window-sill,

Lifted the window sash with care,
  Then, gaily throwing aside the blind,
  Shouted. It was a shock to find
That he was not remembered there.

At once he felt not all his pain,
  But murmuringly apologised,
  Turned, once more sought the undersized
Blown trees, and the long lanky lane,

Wondering and pondering on, past where
  A lamp before him glanced and stayed
  Across his path, so that his shade
Seemed like a giant's moving there.

'ALL THE HILLS AND VALES ALONG'

All the hills and vales along
Earth is bursting into song,
And the singers are the chaps
Who are going to die perhaps,
  O sing, marching men,
  Till the valleys ring again.
  Give your gladness to earth's keeping,
  So be glad, when you are sleeping.

Cast away regret and rue,
Think what you are marching to.
Little live, great pass.
Jesus Christ and Barabbas
Were found the same day.
This died, that went his way.
  So sing with joyful breath,
  For why, you are going to death.
  Teeming earth will surely store
  All the gladness that you pour.

Earth that never doubts nor fears,
Earth that knows of death, not tears,
Earth that bore with joyful ease
Hemlock for Socrates,
Earth that blossomed and was glad
'Neath the cross that Christ had,
Shall rejoice and blossom too
When the bullet reaches you.
  Wherefore, men marching
  On the road to death, sing!
  Pour your gladness on earth's head,
  So be merry, so be dead.

From the hills and valleys earth
Shouts back the sound of mirth,
Tramp of feet and lilt of song
Ringing all the road along.
All the music of their going,
Ringing swinging glad song-throwing,
Earth will echo still, when foot
Lies numb and voice mute.
  On, marching men, on
  To the gates of death with song.
  Sow your gladness for earth's reaping,
  So you may be glad, though sleeping.
  Strew your gladness on earth's bed,
  So be merry, so be dead.

TO GERMANY

You are blind like us. Your hurt no man designed,
And no man claimed the conquest of your land.
But gropers both through fields of thought confined
We stumble and we do not understand.
You only saw your future bigly planned,
And we, the tapering paths of our own mind,
And in each other's dearest ways we stand,
And hiss and hate. And the blind fight the blind.

When it is peace, then we may view again
With new-won eyes each other's truer form
And wonder. Grown more loving-kind and warm
We'll grasp firm hands and laugh at the old pain,
When it is peace. But until peace, the storm
The darkness and the thunder and the rain.

EXPECTANS EXPECTAVI

From morn to midnight, all day through,
I laugh and play as others do,
I sin and chatter, just the same
As others with a different name.

And all year long upon the stage
I dance and tumble and do rage
So vehemently, I scarcely see
The inner and eternal me.

I have a temple I do not
Visit, a heart I have forgot,
A self that I have never met,
A secret shrine—and yet, and yet

This sanctuary of my soul
Unwitting I keep white and whole,
Unlatched and lit, if Thou should'st care
To enter or to tarry there.

With parted lips and outstretched hands
And listening ears Thy servant stands,
Call Thou early, call Thou late,
To Thy great service dedicate.

May 1915

TWO SONNETS

I

Saints have adored the lofty soul of you.
Poets have whitened at your high renown.
We stand among the many millions who
Do hourly wait to pass your pathway down.
You, so familiar, once were strange: we tried
To live as of your presence unaware.
But now in every road on every side
We see your straight and steadfast signpost there.

I think it like that signpost in my land,
Hoary and tall, which pointed me to go
Upward, into the hills, on the right hand,
Where the mists swim and the winds shriek and
    blow,
A homeless land and friendless, but a land
I did not know and that I wished to know.

II

Such, such is Death: no triumph: no defeat:
Only an empty pail, a slate rubbed clean,
A merciful putting away of what has been.

And this we know: Death is not Life effete,
Life crushed, the broken pail. We who have seen
So marvellous things know well the end not yet.

Victor and vanquished are a-one in death:
Coward and brave: friend, foe. Ghosts do not say
'Come, what was your record when you drew
    breath?'
But a big blot has hid each yesterday
So poor, so manifestly incomplete.
And your bright Promise, withered long and sped,
Is touched, stirs, rises, opens and grows sweet
And blossoms and is you, when you are dead.

12 June 1915

'THERE IS SUCH CHANGE IN ALL THOSE FIELDS'

There is such change in all those fields,
Such motion rhythmic, ordered, free,
Where ever-glancing summer yields
Birth, fragrance, sunlight, immanency,
To make us view our rights of birth.
What shall we do? How shall we die?
We, captives of a roaming earth,
'Mid shades that life and light deny.
Blank summer's surfeit heaves in mist;
Dumb earth basks dewy-washed; while still
We whom Intelligence has kissed
Do make us shackles of our will.
And yet I know in each loud brain,
Round-clamped with laws and learning so,
Is madness more and lust of strain
Than earth's jerked godlings e'er can know.
The false Delilah of our brain
Has set us round the millstone going.
O lust of roving! lust of pain!
Our hair will not be long in growing.
Like blinded Samson round we go.
We hear the grindstone groan and cry.
Yet we are kings, we know, we know.
What shall we do? How shall we die?
Take but our pauper's gift of birth,
O let us from the grindstone free!
And tread the maddening gladdening earth
In strength close-braced with purity.
The earth is old; we ever new.
Our eyes should see no other sense
Than this, eternally to DO—
Our joy, our task, our recompense;
Up unexploréd mountains move,
Track tireless through great wastes afar,

Nor slumber in the arms of love,
Nor tremble on the brink of war;
Make Beauty and make Rest give place,
Mock Prudence loud—and she is gone,
Smite Satisfaction on the face
And tread the ghost of Ease upon.
Light-lipped and singing press we hard
Over old earth which now is worn,
Triumphant, buffeted and scarred,
By billows howled at, tempest-torn,
Toward blue horizons far away
(Which do not give the rest we need,
But some long strife, more than this play,
Some task that will be stern indeed)—
We ever new, we ever young,
We happy creatures of a day!
What will the gods say, seeing us strung
As nobly and as taut as they?

TO J.B.

I have not brought my Odyssey
With me here across the sea;
But you'll remember, when I say
How, when they went down Sparta way,
To sandy Sparta, long ere dawn
Horses were harnessed, rations drawn,
Equipment polished sparkling bright,
And breakfasts swallowed (as the white
Of eastern heavens turned to gold)—
The dogs barked, swift farewells were told.
The sun springs up, the horses neigh,
Crackles the whip thrice—then away!

From sun-go-up to sun-go-down
All day across the sandy down
The gallant horses galloped, till
The wind across the downs more still

Blew, the sun sank and all the road
Was darkened, that it only showed
Right at the end the town's red light
And twilight glimmering into night.
The horses never slackened till
They reached the doorway and stood still.
Then came the knock, the unlocking; then
The honey-sweet converse of men,
The splendid bath, the change of dress,
Then–oh the grandeur of their Mess,
The henchmen, the prim stewardess!
And oh the breaking of old ground,
The tales, after the port went round!
(The wondrous wiles of old Odysseus,
Old Agamemnon and his misuse
Of his command, and that young chit
Paris–who didn't care a bit
For Helen–only to annoy Pa
He did it really, *κ.τ.λ.*)

But soon they led amidst the din
The honey-sweet *ἀοιδὸς* in,
Whose eyes were blind, whose soul had sight,
Who knew the fame of men in fight,
Bard of white hair and trembling foot,
Who sang whatever God might put
Into his heart.
And there he sung,
Those war-worn veterans among,
Tales of great war and strong hearts wrung,
Of clash of arms, of council's brawl,
Of beauty that must early fall,
Of battle hate and battle joy
By the old windy walls of Troy.

They felt that they were unreal then,
Visions and shadow-forms, not men.
But those the bard did sing and say

(Some were their comrades, some were they)
Took shape and loomed and strengthened more
Greatly than they had guessed of yore.

* * *

And now the fight begins again,
The old war-joy, the old war-pain,
Sons of one school across the sea
We have no fear to fight, for we
Have echo of our deeds in you
We have our ἀοιδὸς too.

And soon, O soon, I do not doubt it,
With the body or without it,
We shall all come tumbling down
To our old wrinkled red-capped town.
Perhaps the road up Ilsley way,
The old ridge-track, will be my way.
High up among the sheep and sky,
Look down on Wantage, passing by,
And see the smoke from Swindon town:
And then full left at Liddington,
Where the four winds of heaven meet
The earth-blest traveller to greet.
And then my face is toward the south,
There is a singing on my mouth:
Away to rightward I descry
My Barbury ensconced in sky,
Far underneath, the Ogbourne twins,
And at my feet the thyme and whins,
The grasses with their little crowns
Of gold, the lovely Aldbourne downs,
And that old signpost (well I knew
That crazy signpost, arms askew,
Old mother of the four grass ways).
And then my mouth is dumb with praise,
For, past the wood and chalkpit tiny,
A glimpse of Marlborough ἐρατεινή!
So I descend beneath the rail

To warmth and welcome and wassail,
And you, our minstrel, you our bard,
Who makes war's grievous things and hard,
Lightsome and glorious and fair
Will be, at least in spirit, there.
We'll read your rhymes, and we will sing
The toun o' touns till the roofs ring.
And if you'll come among us, then
We shall be most blest of men,
We shall forget the old old pain,
Remember Marlborough again
And hearken all the tales you tell
And bless our old ἀοιδὸς.
Well,
This for the future. Now we stand
Stronger through you, to guard our land,
I do but give the thanks of each
(Thanks far far greater than my speech)
Of those you knew or did not know
(For all knew you) not long ago
In places that we see in sleep
Our eyes are dry but our hearts weep
Warm living tears that memory dear
Calls up the moment that we hear
(For we do hear it) your kind voice
Who understood us, men and boys.
So now and for the ages through
We are all dead and living too.
Our common life lies on your tongue
For as the bards sang, you have sung.

This from the battered trenches–rough,
Jingling and tedious enough.
And so I sign myself to you:
One, who some crooked pathways knew
Round Bedwyn: who could scarcely leave
The Downs on a December eve:
Was at his happiest in shorts,

And got—not many good reports!
Small skill of rhyming in his hand—
But you'll forgive—you'll understand.

12 July 1915

IN MEMORIAM

S.C.W., V.C.

There is no fitter end than this.
  No need is now to yearn nor sigh.
We know the glory that is his,
  A glory that can never die.

Surely we knew it long before,
  Knew all along that he was made
For a swift radiant morning, for
  A sacrificing swift night-shade.

8 September 1915

'WHEN YOU SEE MILLIONS OF THE MOUTHLESS DEAD'

When you see millions of the mouthless dead
Across your dreams in pale battalions go,
Say not soft things as other men have said,
That you'll remember. For you need not so.
Give them not praise. For, deaf, how should they know
It is not curses heaped on each gashed head?
Nor tears. Their blind eyes see not your tears flow.
Nor honour. It is easy to be dead.
Say only this, 'They are dead.' Then add thereto,
'Yet many a better one has died before.'
Then, scanning all the o'ercrowded mass, should you
Perceive one face that you loved heretofore,
It is a spook. None wears the face you knew.
Great death has made all his for evermore.

SELECTED LETTERS
1911 - 1915

1911

TO PROFESSOR AND MRS. SORLEY

Marlborough College,
10 December 1911

On Tuesday we went to Devizes Barracks for the oral examination. There were thirty of us and two brakes to take us—the drive is twelve miles. We started off at nine o'clock in uniform and O.T.C. greatcoats (most comfortable things), with Sergt-Major Barnes (wot we didn't tip) and not (thank Heaven!) the Major to look after us. I got a pew next Barnes and I was sure of an interesting drive. We left the Bath Road at Beckhampton, near Avebury, about six miles from Marlborough, and the scenery, commonplace up till then, opened out and we were soon rolling over the wildest expanse of down I have ever seen. Then Sergt-Major found his true form. Two miles past Beckhampton he asked us to look round. Was there any sign of human habitation in sight? The day was misty and we could see nothing but downs and the road. On this spot, he told us, on this road, about 100 years ago, the Royal Mail had been attacked by a gang of highwaymen. They had killed the driver, made a thorough search of the mail-sacks, taken all that was valuable, and proceeded in the direction of Beckhampton. On the way they met a labourer of Devizes who had been to Beckhampton for some work and—presumably successful on his errand—was returning intoxicated. Him they stunned at a blow and carried back to the wrecks of the mail-cart and the dead driver. They put a pistol in his hand, and laid him unconscious beside the driver's corpse: and they scattered over the country. Next day there were no letters in the West of England, and early goers along the Devizes road had brought information of a wrecked mail-coach, clear signs of a scuffle, stunned horses, a driver shot through the head, and his murderer beside him, stunned, with the fatal pistol. The evidence seemed conclusive—and the wretched labourer was condemned to death.

At this moment a tall and dark farmhouse loomed into sight: 'That,' said Sergt-Major, 'was once Devizes gaol, on that small hillock to the right were once the gallows.' Then he told us to look straight ahead. In front lay miles and miles, as it seemed, of downs: but right at the edge, on the very horizon, a statue of a man on a horse facing towards us. 'It was on a misty December morning like this,' he went on, 'when the man was had out to be hung: the usual crowd of people had assembled: and he was led up to the gallows. He was already standing there looking westwards, when suddenly he lifted up his voice and said, 'I was born and have lived forty years in these parts, and have always seen the statue of one man on horseback; look westward, for to-day there are two.' The crowd, the priest, the sheriff and the hangman looked to the west: there were two men on horseback facing towards them: then the mist thickened and the sight was blotted out. A short consultation followed; they decided the thing was a delusion: the wretch was strung up on the gallows: the crowd dispersed, and his corpse was left hanging in the mist.

'Half an hour later from a direction due westward, a breathless horseman arrived through the mist—now thickened to a fog—at Devizes gaol. In his hand he held a reprieve for Walter Leader, labourer of Devizes, wrongfully convicted of the murder of Henry Castles, driver of the Royal Mail. There had been a quarrel in the gang of highwaymen, one had turned king's evidence at Bath, and a rider had been sent post-haste to Devizes over the downs with the news. They took the body down from the gallows, and under the only tree for two miles round by the side of the main road they buried him. And,' concluded Sergt-Major, 'look to your lefts, gentlemen, please; there is his grave.' We looked to our left. There was one of those crooked trees—the kind we used to say were witches—by the side of the road breaking the monotony; underneath was a mound, six feet long, and a cross at the foot and the head.

Devizes Barracks are up on a hill, a mile this side of Devizes. Apparently we were late, so we dismounted as quickly as possible. The examination is divided into three parts—Company Drill, Tactical and Musketry; for each part the full is 100, and to pass one must get at least 50 in each subject and at least 180 in the whole. We were divided into three groups so that all three portions could proceed simultaneously. My lot was Musketry first, of which I was glad as lack of time has forced me to take it practically unseen. There was a horrible dark little rabbit-hutch, concealing a gawky subaltern with a rifle. We went there one after another alone, and an air of sanctity hung over the whole proceeding. I entered with fear and trembling. Twenty questions I was asked, and I looked sheepish and I said 'Don't know' to each one. Then he said, 'Is there anything you do know?' and I gave him the two pieces of knowledge I had come armed with—the weight of a rifle and episodes in the life of a bullet from the time it leaves the breech till it hits its man. Then I saluted really smartly, and the gentleman gave me 60 out of a hundred. Company Drill came next which merely consisted in drilling a Company (as you might think) of most alarmingly smart regulars. For this I got 70 (every one got 70)—and then I went off to Tactical. Tactical was equally a farce. I was told to send out an advance-guard, lost my head, sent out a flank-guard, scored 70 per cent. I only pray that the examiners in the written exam. are as lenient.

I will not begin dilating on the lunch, first because it would show how greedy I am and secondly because I would never stop. I felt it doing me good all the way home.

After lunch we went over the barracks. I had thought that a Tommy's life was one of comparative hardship. But at Devizes I was disillusioned. They are fed twice as well as we are at Marlborough—bacon every morning for breakfast, and eggs for tea and as much butter and jam as they like. Sergeant B. was speechless with indignation at the pampering they now get. When he was in the same barracks 20 years ago, he had existed for weeks on end on 'skilly,' *i.e.*, dry bread soaked with tea, for these two meals: if they wanted even butter they had to buy it for themselves; and now butter, jam, bacon and eggs at the State's expense. Their dormitories are just like ours, only the beds fold up and they have to do their own dirty work. Though the mess-rooms smell of dirty plates, and the dormitories of beds that are never aired, they have two most magnificent billiard-rooms with full-sized tables, a well-filled library and reading-room, and a very up-to-date gymnasium, all, of course, since Sergt-Major's time and all very extravagant. They have two soccer grounds—one quite level—and a bathing place in the canal. So I should not think they have much to complain of.

They were very interesting to watch—those Wiltshire Tommies: not one of them, I should say, above 5 ft. 8 in height, and precious few of them less than 40 round the chest: short, thick, sturdy fellows, fair-haired for the most part and red-faced and, when once parade was over, very merry but very shy.

We left the barracks about 2.30: only three people had been ploughed—they must have been bad. It was a very fine afternoon and a good drive home. I only wish they had not been so kind in marking me so that I might have tried again in the summer. I quite envy the three failures.

1913

TO PROFESSOR AND MRS. SORLEY

Marlborough College,
27 January 1913

I have been having an exciting time talking to various ushers all to-day about various things. I wanted (and still want) to give up Classics, but they were very patient and talked me round. I find Classics more and more boring every day; but Dyson (the Music Master) after a long talk showed me that it was far best to keep it on and go up to the University (which I have never wanted to do, in secret), and that was the only way to get a kind of Alexander-Paterson post, which is the career I have always wanted. I had a mad idea, precipitated by a row with Atkey at the beginning of the term, of chucking Classics, leaving and becoming an Elementary Schoolmaster—with an utter ignorance of how to do so. Dyson (who knows a lot about it having done that kind of work himself) pointed [out] that that would defeat its own end, and that the only way to get that kind of career I wish was to keep on with Classics and go up to the Varsity—merely as a means to an end. After taking my degree (I would not in that case need to stay four years), it would be easy to get a post at a night-school or working-man's college: but that was the only way to get at that kind of career. While up at Oxford, he showed me, I could make a beginning by working at Oxford House, and, after I had got a scholarship, there would be no pressing need to continue those detestable Classics in the detestably serious spirit demanded. I could spend a lot of time in social work and make a beginning then.

This is no new idea of mine—to become an instructor in a Working Man's College or something of that sort. Why I didn't tell you before I don't know. But until to-day it was only a hazy dream—I had no idea of how or when to do it. But now that Dyson has given me facts, it seems much nearer than before. And it will mean staying on here, as in any case, and going up for a scholarship at Oxford, just as if I had been going in for the Indian Civil Service. I did not foresee that, and thought I should have to leave and go straight into it, which would have been more satisfactory, but is, as Dyson showed, utterly impracticable. I feel much more easy now, except that I doubt that it is really good my staying on here at any rate after I go up for a scholarship. When one reaches the top of a public school, one has such unbounded opportunities of getting unbearably conceited that I don't see how anyone survives the change that must come when the tin god is swept off his little kingdom and becomes an unimportant mortal again. And besides I am sure it is far too enjoyable, and one is awfully tempted to pose all the time and be theatrical. But still, till the end of this year, I suppose I had better stay on, *i.e.,* till scholarship time. Of course I want to awfully—that is the chief reason against it. The next four years have got to be bridged over somehow, and I had better bridge them in the conventional and, I suppose, the best way till I am able to enter the career I have always wanted since I read *Across the Bridges* in the courtyard of the Unicorn Inn.

I ought to have explained all this before. But somehow—you'll understand—one hates talking (I know it's only silly shy self-consciousness) about anything one really feels. These things go much better into ink. But I hope you agree that the best thing is to go in for a schol. which can take me up to Oxford (Dyson says Oxford offers much more opportunities that way: he is unbiassed having been at neither), and, after taking my degree, he says there will be no difficulty in obtaining the kind of post I want. There are objections to this. A year more of downright hard Classics is not a pleasant prospect. And a year more of being a little tin god is alarmingly and disastrously alluring. But Dyson assures me it is the best and only way—though four years is a long time to wait. But if ever I forget the kindness of Dyson, I ought to be knocked down!

So now I feel clearer. What I have wanted in secret has become realisable and without any change in my routine at present. I hope you are not angry that I did not tell you before that the idea of India was always a bit of a bogey to me: I shouldn't suit the life at all.

1914

TO THE MASTER OF MARLBOROUGH

Schwerin in Mecklenburg
20 February 1914

I have been here a lunar month to-day: up to date I have done no Classics whatsoever: to-morrow I intend to begin: and I think there could be no more suitable time than the eve of my reformation, for reporting myself to you.

I am admirably pleased with myself, and consequently with everyone else. I can now meet all the members of the family with which I am staying on equal terms, and we discuss the deepest subjects, such as the English Public School system, and often understand what the other has to say. The Frau, who gives me lessons, I see most of. I began, in my way, by despising her utterly. Now all that is changed, and, to use the Irish expression, 'Me to live a hundred years, I would never be tired of praising'—at least, I hope not. She has also a delightful little brother of 23, who is very nice to me. He is a student of sorts, and on account of his industry had earned the title of the Bookworm, till I came, I, whose industry was never appreciated at Marlborough, and (Gospel Truth) usurped that title.

But what has given me most pleasure is the existence of a Hockey Club in Schwerin. I hope you will not think me ungrateful, but I enjoy hockey here ten times more than I did in your kingdom. You know I am not given to boasting, but, though I say it as shouldn't, I *know* I am far the best outside-right within ten miles round. Now in Marlborough they never thought that of me. Yes, hockey means a different thing than that cold-blooded performance on winter evenings beneath the eyes of an Officious and Offensive House-captain, that it used to mean. We now play twice a week, beginning at three o'clock and continuing till the sun goes down and 'Εσπέρα πάντα φέρων drives us in darkness to bed. This Season (I think that is the proper word) I have already scored 37 goals (incidentally, the first 37 goals of my career), and when the modest blushing Invincible Outside Right is congratulated at the close of the game on his skill (yes, skill), he explains in broken German, that at the school in England he was considered a contemptible performer, and they open their eyes like Dick Whittington and think with reverence on the School, where Talent at Hockey is as cheap as Gold Nuggets in Eldorado. At least, I don't suppose they really do.

The only objection I have to make is about the absence of shorts: or perhaps I should say (the former might be misunderstood) the rule that nice gentlemanly knickerbockers that conceal the knees must be worn. The three German officers that belong to the club play in their Sunday clothes—boiled shirts, butterflies and spats. They have not yet hit the ball, but are still trying. Now isn't that delightful? Catch a beastly English officer making a public donkey of himself! I think it is the utter absence of self-consciousness that makes the Germans so much nicer than the English.

For just at present, my patriotism is on leave. I cannot imagine a nicer nation. I was coming back from a long walk with the Frau last night and we passed a couple of companies of military returning from a field day of sorts. It is truth that we could hear them a mile off. Were they singing? They were roaring—something glorious and senseless about the Fatherland (in England it would have been contemptible Jingo: it wasn't in Deutschland), and all the way home we heard the roar, and when they neared the town the echo was tremendous. Two hundred lungs all bellowing. And when I got home, I felt I was a German, and proud to be a German: when the tempest of the singing was at its loudest, I felt that perhaps I could die for Deutschland—and I have never had an inkling of that feeling about England, and never shall. And if the feeling died with the cessation of the singing—well I had it, and it's the first time I have had the vaguest idea what patriotism meant—and that in a strange land. Nice, isn't it?

And the language is so glorious. Thoughts that appear vapid or sentimental in English, are glorious when clothed in German. That's what I find. My attempts to translate have met with no success. I have been to the theatre here and seen Ibsen's *John Gabriel Borkman* magnificently acted. In English, the play would be wizened. These magnificent compound words! The prodigal will find his return to the defunct languages to-morrow a wet-blankety job.

I cannot regret for one moment having left. The temporary loss of many friends is entirely compensated for by the eternal discovery of a language. It is such a relief, too, to be clear of any artificial position of responsibility, which continually threatens to make one a prig, a poser, or a censor. All temptations to be always striving in the race of showing off, are gone. For try and show off here, and you get short shrift. One day, a little annoyed by the German honesty in not concealing the natural human love of food, I said, 'it didn't matter to me what I ate. All food was alike to me.' When we came in to Abendessen that evening, the rest of the family had the usual nice meal, but I was only given bread and butter—as much bread and butter as I liked—but as it was all the same to me, nothing more. It was not long before I withdrew my silly statement, and helped myself to sausage.

I have a kind of feeling that towards the end of January I left

Egypt and arrived safely in Canaan. I know it's wrong, but if you had heard those soldiers singing

> Vaterland, mein Vaterland,
> Es giebt auf wiedersehen!

you would have felt the same.

TO PROFESSOR AND MRS. SORLEY

Jena,
26 July 1914

The haystack has caught fire. The drunken Verbindungen are parading the streets shouting 'Down with the Serbs.' Every half-hour, even in secluded Jena, comes a fresh edition of the papers, each time with wilder rumours: so that one can almost hear the firing at Belgrade. But perhaps this is only a German sabbatical liveliness. At any rate, it seems that Russia must to-night settle the question of a continental war, or no. Curious that an Austrian-Servian war—the one ideal of the late Austrian Crown-prince's life—should be attained first by his death. It puts him on a level with the heroes:

> Erst, wenn er sterben muss an diesem Stern,
> Sehen wir dass er an diesem Stern gelebt—

as Rilke says of Christ. . . .

TO A. E. HUTCHINSON

Cambridge, 10 (?) August 1914

I daresay that, after the three years that Lord K. has allotted for the war, they'll forward me from Jena a letter from you written to me about this time. Howbeit, even supposing you sent one loose into that delightful land, I naturally never received it. For, after I had spent three splendid days trying to make Hopper drunk with Mosel wine in the Mosel valley (I never got him further than the state of 'not drunk but having drink taken'), they took us up as spies and put us into prison at Trier. To be exact, the 'imprisonment' only lasted 8½ hours; but

I was feeling a real prisoner by the time they let us out. I had a white cell, a bowl of soup, a pitcher of solidifying water, a hole in the wall through which I talked to the prisoner next door, a prison bed, a prison bible: so altogether they did the thing in style. We had also a hissing crowd shouting 'Totschiessen' to accompany us from the barracks to the prison. It couldn't have been arranged more finely: and the man who had occupied the cell before me had just been taken out and shot for being a Frenchman. But the English were in high favour, and I started a rumour that England had declared war on Russia; so they readily gave us a dismissal at our examination, and a free pass calling us unsuspicious. We travelled slowly to Cologne all through Sunday night: but a sad thing happened there, and Paul and Barnabas parted. Barnabas went on in the same train to Amsterdam hoping thereby to reach Hook; while Paul (ravenous for breakfast) 'detrained' at Cologne and had a huge meal. I, of course, was Paul.

Meanwhile your post-card has arrived and many thanks. I explain. Your letter probably reached Jena after I had left and was forwarded to the Poste Restante, Trier, as I had directed. But the only three public buildings I was allowed to see were the barracks, the prison, and the station. So, as I have said before, I shall send for the letter and post-cards in three years. They have probably read your letter at Trier and cut out with scissors the words they consider improper.

To proceed, as Sergt-Major Barnes says. I took a train to Brussels, but they turned me out at a deserted village on the Belgian frontier. I walked to the next town and took train sorrowfully to Brussels. At Brussels I had 'financial difficulties' and had to call on half the consuls in the place to solve them, and then I travelled sordidly on to Antwerp. The last ship had sailed for Harwich so the English consul chartered an old broken-down sad ship called the 'Montrose'. It was being embalmed in Antwerp Harbour because Miss le Neve had been taken prisoner on board it four years ago. They gave us Capt. Kendall, who was last seen going down with the 'Empress of Ireland,' to take command. And after three days' journey with commercial travellers of the most revoltingly John Bullish description, I got home on Thursday and was mistaken for the gardener. He always wears my worn-out clo's, so we are constantly interchanged. But mark. Hopper, who arrived triumphant at Harwich two days before I did, had to pay for his crossing. I got a free passage as far as London, where I borrowed money from my aunt's butler to take me on to Cambridge; and my aunt repaid the debt.

Now, have you ever heard a more commonplace and sordid narrative? At least I found it so in experience—merely dull, after I had left Hopper. The only bright star was a drunken Austrian, with whom we travelled from Trier to Coblenz, who seated himself opposite to us and gazed in our faces and at last said lovingly: 'Ihr seid gewiss Hamburger Jungen.' The poor man was trying to go from Kiel to Vienna, and, perpetually drunken, had travelled via Brussels, Paris, Marseilles, and Metz, which even you must know is not the shortest way. After he had flung Hopper's cap out of the window, he said that Hopper was a 'feiner Mann,' but said nothing about me, which just shows how drunk he was. But otherwise it was dull. Now, behold, I cannot stir out of the house, but some lady friend of my mother's, whose mind is upset by the present business, rushes up and says 'O, you're the boy that's had such *adventures*. Been in prison too, I hear. You *must* come and tell us all about it.' Then there's aunts to be written to. I shall probably be driven into writing a book 'Across Germany in an O.M. tie' or 'Prison Life in Germany by one who has seen it,' followed shortly by another entitled: 'Three days on the open sea with Commercial Travellers' or 'Britannia Rules the Waves.' And so I am simply nauseated by the memory of these five very ordinary and comparatively dull days. The preceeding days in the Moselthal were far nicer: only Hopper was so provincial, and, when I entered a Gasthaus with a knowing swagger and said 'I wish to sample the local Mosel here; what vintage do you recommend?' Hopper would burst in with 'Haben Sie Münchener Bier?' and a huge grin on his face: unwitting what a heinous sin it is to order beer in a wine district. So we generally compromized on hot milk.

Having proved my identity at home as distinct from the

gardener's, I investigated my (a-hem!) 'papers' and found, among old receipts for college clothes and such like, a lovely piece of paper, which I daresay you have got too, which dismissed me from the corps. Only mine had EXCELLENT written (in the Major's hand) for my General Efficiency. Yours can have had, at most, 'very good.' I took this down to a man of sorts and said 'Mit Gott für Kaiser und Vaterland, I mean, für König und Mutterland: what can I do to have some reasonable answer to give to my acquaintances when they ask me, "What are *you* doing?"?' He looked me up and down and said, 'Send in for a commission in the Territorials. You may get something there. You'll get an answer in a fortnight's time, not before.' Compromise as usual. Not heroic enough to do the really straight thing and join the regulars as a Tommy, I have made a stupid compromise [with] my conscience and applied for a commission in the Terriers, where no new officers are wanted. In a month's time I shall probably get the beastly thing: and spend the next twelve months binding the corn, guarding the bridges, frightening the birds away, and otherwise assisting in Home Defence. So I think you were sensible to prefer your last term at Marlborough. Only I wish you could come and join the beastly battalion of Cambridgeshire clerks to which I shall be tacked on: and we could sow the corn and think we were soldiers together.

But isn't all this bloody? I am full of mute and burning rage and annoyance and sulkiness about it. I could wager that out of twelve million eventual combatants there aren't twelve who really want it. And 'serving one's country' is so unpicturesque and unheroic when it comes to the point. Spending a year in a beastly Territorial camp guarding telegraph wires has nothing poetical about it: nor very useful as far as I can see. Besides the Germans are so nice; but I suppose the best thing that could happen to them would be their defeat.

At present I am sitting still here with no clothes (my luggage being all in Germany), swearing mildly under my breath and sulking. There is absolutely nothing to be done, and if I hadn't been a coward I should have joined the Regulars. As it is, I still have decent food and my rubber of bridge every evening; and, as long as I am not supposed to be 'telling my adventures' and making sport for the Philistines, things are quite nice and dull. But there's no getting round it, it's a damned nuisance. I shall get off Oxford for a year, however, which is one blessing. Of course I am regarding the whole thing from an egoistic point of view. But, when everyone else is being so splendidly patriotic, that 'Wille zu Widerspruch' or cussedness, which is chief among my (few) vices, is making me, since I cannot be actively pro-German, merely sulky.

Having written fifteen pages exclusively about myself, I'd better stop. Yours was the first post-card which has come to this house in the last week which did not say 'We are cutting down bacon and *so* amused trying to work out little economies. Now, what are *you* doing?' Therefor thanks. I think at this time of national financial difficulties that, if a fine were put on the use of the word 'God' in connection with this catastrophe in private correspondence (such as 'Good God,' 1*d*., 'Please God,' 1*s*., 'Pray God,' 1*s*. 6*d*., these being just interjections; but remarks as 'Truly God's ways are inscrutable, he is great,' 2 guineas, and 'God never meant,' £100)—I think we would then raise a large amount of the indemnity which we shall undoubtedly have to pay in a year or two years' time. We have had so many such letters. Also all remarks about the Emperor being mad, 10*s*.6*d*. I often think that if talking about the war were altogether forbidden it would be good. Our friends and correspondents don't seem to be able to give up physical luxuries without indulging in emotional luxuries as compensation. But I'm thankful to see that Kipling hasn't written a poem yet.

Well, I was very sorry to miss your letter and the subsequent horde of post-cards. But, in spite of your civilian attitude, I hope you are flourishing: unless God (5*s*.) thinks fit to punish your lack of patriotism by sending a murrain among the horses on the Tudhoe acres. I am too helplessly angry still to write coherently. Complete comfort is out of the question, and I like complete comfort.

TO A. J. HOPKINSON

Shorncliffe, October (?) 1914

I thought the enclosure from [your] Uncle peculiarly interesting and return as you must want to keep it. He put the case for Prussian (as distinct from German) efficiency far more fairly than I had ever thought of it before. I think his trans-atlantic criticism of England's 'imaginative indolence' and consequent social rottenness most stimulating in this time of auto-trumpeting and Old-England-she's-the-same-as-ever-isms. Also I suppose he is to a certain extent right that we have temporarily renounced all our claim to the more articulate and individual parts of our individuality. But in the intervals of doing and dying let's speak to one another as two pro-Germans, or nearly so, who have tramped her roads, bathed in her Moselles, and spent half-a-day in her cells.

The two great sins people impute to Germany are that she says that might is right and bullies the little dogs. But I don't think that she means might *qua* might is right, but that confidence of superiority is right, and by superiority she means spiritual superiority. She said to Belgium, 'We enlightened thinkers see that it is necessary to the world that all opposition to Deutsche Kultur should be crushed. As citizens of the world you must assist us in our object and assert those higher ideas of world-citizenship which are not bound by treaties. But if you oppose us, we have only one alternative.' That, at least, is what the best of them would have said; only the diplomats put it rather more brusquely. She was going on a missionary voyage with all the zest of Faust—

> Er wandle so den Erdentag entlang;
> Wenn Geister spuken, geh' er seinen Gang;
> Im Weiterschreiten find' er Qual und Glück,
> Er, unbefriedigt jeden Augenblick!

—and missionaries know no law. As Uncle Alder says, her Kultur (in its widest sense) is the best in the world: so she must scatter it broadcast through the world perforce, saying like the schoolmaster or the dentist 'though it hurts at present, it'll do you no end of good afterwards.' (Perhaps she will even have to add at the end of the war 'and it's hurt me more than it's hurt you.')

So it seems to me that Germany's only fault (and I think you often commented on it in those you met) is a lack of real insight and sympathy with those who differ from her. We are not fighting a bully, but a bigot. They are a young nation and don't yet see that what they consider is being done for the good of the world may be really being done for self-gratification —like X. who, under pretence of informing the form, dropped into the habit of parading his own knowledge. X. incidentally did the form a service by creating great amusement for it, and so is Germany incidentally doing the world a service (though not in the way it meant) by giving them something to live and die for, which no country but Germany had before. If the bigot conquers he will learn in time his mistaken methods (for it is only of the methods and not of the goal of Germany that one can disapprove)—just as the early Christian bigots conquered by bigotry and grew larger in sympathy and tolerance after conquest. I regard the war as one between sisters, between Martha and Mary, the efficient and intolerant against the casual and sympathetic. Each side has a virtue for which it is fighting, and each that virtue's supplementary vice. And I hope that whatever the material result of the conflict, it will purge these two virtues of their vices, and efficiency and tolerance will no longer be incompatible.

But I think that tolerance is the larger virtue of the two, and efficiency must be her servant. So I am quite glad to fight this rebellious servant. In fact I look at it this way. Suppose my platoon were the world. Then my platoon-sergeant would represent efficiency and I would represent tolerance. And I always take the sternest measures to keep my platoon-sergeant in check! I fully appreciate the wisdom of the War Office when they put inefficient officers to rule sergeants....

1915

TO A. E. HUTCHINSON

Shorncliffe, 25 January 1915

How are you getting on? I can imagine it is not quite heaven. But neither is this. Heaven will have to wait until the war's over. It is the most asphyxiating work after the first fine glow of seeing people twice your age and size obey and salute you has passed off, as it does after a fortnight. The only thing is that the pay is good. The rest, as you are probably finding already, is complete stagnation among a mass of straps and sleeping-bags and water-bottles. War in England only means putting all the men of 'military age' in England into a state of routinal coma, preparatory to getting them killed. You are being given six months to become conventional: your peace thus made with God, you will be sent out and killed. At least, if you aren't killed, you'll come back so unfitted for any other job that you'll have to stay in the Army. I should like so much to kill whoever was primarily responsible for the war. The alarming sameness with which day passes day until this unnatural state of affairs is over is worse than any so-called atrocities; for people enjoy grief, the only unbearable thing is dullness.

I have started to read again, having read nothing all the closing months of last year. I have discovered a man called D.H. Lawrence who knows the way to write, and I still stick to Hardy: to whom I never managed to convert you.

We talk of going out in March. I am positively looking forward to that event, not in the brave British drummer-boy spirit, of course, but as a relief from this boredom (part of which, by the way, is caused through Philpott having been away the last three weeks in hospital).

We don't seem to be winning, do we? It looks like an affair of years. If so, pray God for a nice little bullet wound (tidy and clean) in the shoulder. That's the place.

Sorry I haven't more to write—nor had Lot's wife when she was half through being turned into salt; nor will you in three months' time.

TO MRS. SORLEY

Aldershot, March 1915

We are off for a wild game this week-end under the eyes of Kitchener. But going out still remains an uncertainty as to time, and has become a matter of the indifferent future to most of us. If we had gone out earlier we would have gone out with a thrill in poetic-martial vein: now most of us have become by habit soldiers, at least in so far that we take such things as a matter of course and a part of our day's work that our own anticipations can neither quicken nor delay.

I talked a lot (in her native tongue) to the hostess with whom I was billeted, and her sensible German attitude was like a cold bath. She saw the thing, as German hausfraus would, directly and humanly and righteously. Especially sensible was she in her remarks against the kind ladies who told her she ought to be proud and glad to give her sons to fight. After all, war in this century is inexcusable: and all parties engaged in it must take an equal share in the blame of its occurrence. If only the English from Grey downwards would cease from rubbing in that, in the days that set all the fuel ablaze, they worked for peace honestly and with all their hearts! We know they did; but in the past their lack of openness and trust in their diplomatic relationships helped to pile the fuel to which Germany applied the torch.

I do wish also that people would not deceive themselves by talk of a just war. There is no such thing as a just war. What we are doing is casting out Satan by Satan. When once war was declared the damage was done: and we, in whom that particular Satan was perhaps less strong than in our foes, had only one course, namely to cast out the far greater Satan by means of him: and he must be fought to the bitter end. But that doesn't alter the fact that long ago there should have been an understanding in Europe that any country that wanted Weltmacht might have it. The Allies may yet score a victory over Germany. But by last August they had thrown away their chances of a true victory. I remember you once on the Ellerby moors telling us the story of Bishop What's-his-name and John-Val-John from *Les Misérables*. And now, although we failed then of the highest, we might have fought, regarding the war—not, as we do regard it, as a candle to shed light upon our unselfishness and love of freedom, but—as a punishment for our past presumptuousness. We had the silver candlesticks and brandished them ever proudly as our own, won by our own valour. Germany must be crushed for her wicked and selfish aspiration to be mistress of the world: but the country that, when mistress of the world, failed to set her an example of unworldliness and renunciation should take to herself half the blame of the blood expended in the crushing.

TO MRS. SORLEY

Aldershot, 28 April 1915

I saw Rupert Brooke's death in *The Morning Post. The Morning Post,* which has always hitherto disapproved of him, is now loud in his praises because he has conformed to their stupid axiom of literary criticism that the only stuff of poetry is violent physical experience, by dying on active service. I think Brooke's earlier poems—especially notably *The Fish* and *Grantchester,* which you can find in *Georgian Poetry*—are his best. That last sonnet-sequence of his, of which you sent me the review in the *Times Lit. Sup.*, and which has been so praised, I find (with the exception of that beginning 'These hearts were woven of human joys and cares, Washed marvellously with sorrow' which is not about himself) overpraised. He is far too obsessed with his own sacrifice, regarding the going to war of himself (and others) as a highly intense, remarkable and sacrificial exploit, whereas it is merely the conduct demanded of him (and others) by the turn of circumstances, where non-compliance with this demand would have made life intolerable. It was not that 'they' gave up anything of that list he gives in one sonnet: but that the essence of these things had been endangered by circumstances over which he had no control, and he must fight to recapture them. He has clothed his attitude in fine words: but he has taken the sentimental attitude....

TO PROFESSOR AND MRS. SORLEY

7th Suffolks, 12th Division,
B.E.F., 1 June 1915

I have just been censoring letters: which hardly puts one in a mood for writing. Suffice it that we are in a little hamlet, or rather settlement of farms; the men on straw, the officers in old four-posters: within sound of the guns. Nothing disturbs these people. I have never felt so restful. There is cidre and cidre and cidre to drink, which reminds one of Normandy. And over all hangs the smell of never-lifted manure. It is in a valley—a feature which I did not know existed in Northern France.

The reading of a hundred letters has brought home to me one need. Could you send me out some of those filthy Woodbine cigarettes the men smoke—they all ask for them. Pour moi, I am well provided for the present.

So far our company are separated from the rest. It is like a picnic, and the weather is of the best.

TO ARTHUR WATTS

1 June 1915

Having begun in ink I continue in pencil. Schottische Sparsamkeit. You aren't worth ink. Besides ink hardly gives that impression of strenuous campaigning I am wishful to produce.

'Also,' this is a little hamlet, smelling pleasantly of manure. I have never felt more restful. We arrived at dawn: white dawn across the plane trees and coming through the fields of rye. After two hours in an oily ship and ten in a grimy train, the 'war area' was a haven of relief. These French trains shriek so: there is no sight more desolating than abandoned engines passing up and down the lines, hooting in their loneliness. There is something eerie in a railway by night.

But this is perfect. The other officers have heard the heavy guns and perhaps I shall soon. They make perfect cider in this valley: still, like them. There are clouds of dust along the roads, and in the leaves: but the dust here is native and caressing and pure, not like the dust of Aldershot, gritted and fouled by motors and thousands of feet. 'Tis a very Limbo lake: set between the tireless railways behind and twenty miles in front the fighting. Drink its cider and paddle in its rushy streams: and see if you care whether you die to-morrow. It brings out a new part of one's self, the loiterer, neither scorning nor desiring delights, gliding listlessly through the minutes from meal-time to meal-time, like the stream through the rushes: or stagnant and smooth like their cider, unfathomably gold: beautiful and calm without mental fear. And in four-score hours we will pull up our braces and fight. These hours will have slipt over me, and I shall march hotly to the firing-line, by turn critic, actor, hero, coward and soldier of fortune: perhaps even for a moment Christian, humble, with 'Thy will be done.' Then shock, combustion, the emergence of one of these: death or life: and then return to the old rigmarole. I imagine that this, while it may or may not knock about your body, will make very little difference to you otherwise.

A speedy relief from Chatham. There is vibration in the air when you hear 'The Battalion will move across the water on.....'

The moon won't rise till late, but there is such placid weariness in all the bearing earth, that I must go out to see. I have not been 'auf dem Lande' for many years: man muss den Augenblick geniessen.

Leb' wohl. I think often of you and Jena: where I was first on my own and found freedom. Leb' wohl.

TO MISS JEAN SORLEY

17 June 1915

This is not like our last visit to France: among other things in that I have to speak more French. But it has this in common—mosquitoes: though we are not otherwise plagued by small living things. Indeed the mosquitoes trouble us far more than brother Bosch. It is difficult to get any real news through. But what I have seen of War so far is this. A cornfield: you think it an ordinary cornfield till you see a long narrow trench at either end: in front of each trench is barbed wire among the corn. You might watch that field all day: and if you were deaf, you would never guess that both of these trenches were filled with foes: you would wonder how those queer underground inhabitants spent their time, and why they dared not show their heads above ground. Only, during the night, troops are constantly shifted: back and forward: north and south. The staff know that a sense of humour won't allow of this sitting face to face in a cornfield for long, without both parties coming out and fraternizing, as happened so constantly a few months ago.

TO MRS. SORLEY

10 July 1915

We have taken over a new lot of trenches and have been having a busy time this past week: our exertions have been those of the navvy rather than those of the soldier. And—without at all 'fraternizing'—we refrain from interfering with Brother Bosch seventy yards away, as long as he is kind to us. So all day there is trench duty broken by feverish letter censoring. No amount of work will break the men's epistolary spirit: I am qualifying for the position of either navvy or post-office clerk after the war. During the night a little excitement is provided by patrolling the enemy's wire. Our chief enemy is nettles and mosquitoes. All patrols—English and German—are much averse to the death and glory principle; so, on running up against one another in the long wet rustling clover, both pretend that they are Levites and the other is a Good Samaritan —and pass by on the other side, no word spoken. For either side to bomb the other would be a useless violation of the unwritten laws that govern the relations of combatants permanently within a hundred yards of distance of each other, who have found out that to provide discomfort for the other is but a roundabout way of providing it for themselves: until they have their heads banged forcibly together by the red-capped powers behind them, whom neither attempts to understand. Meanwhile weather is 'no bon': food, 'plenty bon': temper, fair: sleep, jamais.

Such is 'attrition,' that last resort of paralysed strategy of which we hear so much.

I hate the growing tendency to think that every man drops overboard his individuality between Folkestone and Boulogne, and becomes on landing either 'Tommy' with a character like a nice big fighting pet bear and an incurable yearning and whining for mouth-organs and cheap cigarettes: or the Young Officer with a face like a hero and a silly habit of giggling in the face of death. The kind of man who writes leading articles in *The Morning Post*, and fills the sadly huge gaps in his arguments by stating that the men at the front either all want conscription or think that Haldane should be hanged, is one step worse than [the people] who think that our letters concern our profession and not our interests. 'I hate a fool.'

I should think that that swarm of alliterative busybodies, who see no reason why everyone they meet, and do not take the trouble to 'kennen lernen,' should not be Girl Guides or Women Workers or Lady Lamplighters or whatever the latest craze is, must be almost as annoying to J. as the mother-of-sixteen flies are out here. A pity that she cannot adopt the same method with them as I can with my flies. Still 'kill that fly' would be a crushing retort.

TO PROFESSOR SORLEY

15 July 1915

Your letter, dated 13th, has just arrived. We are now at the end of a few days' rest, a kilometre behind the lines. Except for the farmyard noises (new style) it might almost be the little village that first took us to its arms six weeks ago. It has been a fine day, following on a day's rain, so that the earth smells like spring. I have just managed to break off a long conversation with the farmer in charge, a tall thin stooping man with sad eyes, in trouble about his land: les Anglais stole his peas, trod down his corn and robbed his young potatoes: he told it as a father telling of infanticide. There may have been fifteen francs' worth of damage done; he will never get compensation out of those shifty Belgian burgomasters; but it was not exactly the fifteen francs but the invasion of the soil that had been his for forty years, in which the weather was his only enemy, that gave him a kind of Niobe's dignity to his complaint.

Meanwhile there is the usual evening sluggishness. Close by, a quickfirer is pounding away its allowance of a dozen shells a day. It is like a cow coughing. Eastward there begins a sound (all sounds begin at sundown and continue intermittently till midnight, reaching their zenith at about 9 p.m. and then dying away as sleepiness claims their makers)—a sound like a motor-cycle race—thousands of motor-cycles tearing round and round a track, with cut-outs out: it is really a pair of machine guns firing. And now one sound awakens another. The old cow coughing has started the motor-bikes: and now at intervals of a few minutes come express trains in our direction: you can hear them rushing toward us; they pass going straight for the town behind us: and you hear them begin to slow down as they reach the town: they will soon stop: but no, every time, just before they reach it, is a tremendous railway accident. At least, it must be a railway accident, there is so much noise, and you can see the dust that the wreckage scatters. Sometimes the train behind comes very close, but it too smashes on the wreckage of its forerunners. A tremendous cloud of dust, and then the groans. So many trains and accidents start the cow coughing again: only another cow this time, somewhere behind us, a tremendous-sized cow, *θαυμάσιον ὅσον*, with awful whooping-cough. It must be a buffalo: this cough must burst its sides. And now someone starts sliding down the stairs on a tin tray, to soften the heart of the cow, make it laugh and cure its cough. The din he makes is appalling. He is beating the tray with a broom now, every two minutes a stroke: he has certainly stopped the cow by this time, probably killed it. He will leave off soon (thanks to the 'shell tragedy'): we know he can't last.

It is now almost dark: come out and see the fireworks. While waiting for them to begin you can notice how pale and white the corn is in the summer twilight: no wonder with all this whooping-cough about. And the motor-cycles: notice how all these races have at least a hundred entries: there is never a single cycle going. And why are there no birds coming back to roost? Where is the lark? I haven't heard him all today. He must have got whooping-cough as well, or be staying at home through fear of the cow. I think it will rain to-morrow, but there have been no swallows circling low, stroking their breasts on the full ears of corn. Anyhow, it is night now, but the circus does not close till twelve. Look! there is the first of them! The fireworks are beginning. Red flares shooting up high into the night, or skimming low over the ground, like the swallows that are not: and rockets bursting into stars. See how they illumine that patch of ground a mile in front. See it, it is deadly pale in their searching light: ghastly, I think, and featureless except for two big lines of eyebrows ashy white, parallel along it, raised a little from its surface. Eyebrows. Where are the eyes? Hush, there are no eyes. What those shooting flares illumine is a mole. A long thin mole. Burrowing by day, and shoving a timorous enquiring snout above the ground by night. Look, did you see it? No, you cannot see it from here. But were you a good deal nearer, you would see behind that snout a long and endless row of sharp shining teeth. The rockets catch the light from these teeth and the teeth glitter: they are silently removed from the poison-spitting gums of the mole. For the mole's gums spit fire and, they say, send something more concrete than fire darting into the night. Even when its teeth are off. But you cannot see all this from here: you can only see the rockets and then for a moment the pale ground beneath. But it is quite dark now.

And now for the fun of the fair! You will hear soon the riding-master crack his whip—why, there it is. Listen, a thousand whips are cracking, whipping the horses round the ring. At last! The fun of the circus is begun. For the motor-cycle team race has started off again: and the whips are cracking all: and the waresman starts again, beating his loud tin tray to attract the customers: and the cows in the cattle-show start coughing, coughing: and the firework display is at its best: and the circus specials come one after another bearing the merry-makers back to town, all to the inevitable crash, the inevitable accident. It can't last long: these accidents are so frequent, they'll all get soon killed off, I hope. Yes, it is diminishing. The train service is cancelled (and time too): the cows have stopped coughing: and the cycle race is done. Only the kids who have bought new whips at the fair continue to crack them: and unused rockets that lie about the ground are still sent up occasionally. But now the children are being driven off to bed: only an occasional whip-crack now (perhaps the child is now the sufferer): and the tired showmen going over the ground pick up the rocket-sticks and dead flares. At least I suppose this is what must be happening: for occasionally they still find one that has not yet gone off and send it up out of mere perversity. Else what silence!

It must be midnight now. Yes, it is midnight. But before you go to bed, bend down, put your ear against the ground. What do you hear? 'I hear an endless tapping and a tramping to and fro: both are muffled: but they come from everywhere. Tap, tap, tap: pick, pick, pick: tra-mp, tra-mp, tra-mp.' So you see the circus-goers are not all gone to sleep. There is noise coming from the womb of earth, noise of men who tap and mine and dig and pass to and fro on their watch. What you have seen is the foam and froth of war: but underground is labour and throbbing and long watch. Which will one day bear their fruit. They will set the circus on fire. Then what pandemonium! Let us hope it will not be to-morrow!

TO ARTHUR WATTS

26 August 1915

* * *

Health—and I don't know what ill-health is—invites you so much to smooth and shallow ways: where a happiness may only be found by renouncing the other happiness of which one set out in search. Yet here there is enough to stay the bubbling surface stream. Looking into the future one sees a holocaust somewhere: and at present there is—thank God—enough of 'experience' to keep the wits edged (a callous way of putting it, perhaps). But out in front at night in that no-man's land and long graveyard there is a freedom and a spur. Rustling of the grasses and grave tap-tapping of distant workers: the tension and silence of encounter, when one struggles in the dark for moral victory over the enemy patrol: the wail of the exploded bomb and the animal cries of wounded men. Then death and the horrible thankfulness when one sees that the next man is dead: 'We won't have to *carry* him in under fire, thank God; dragging will do': hauling in of the great resistless body in the dark, the smashed head rattling: the relief, the relief that the thing has ceased to groan: that the bullet or bomb that made the man an animal has now made the animal a corpse. One is hardened by now: purged of all false pity: perhaps more selfish than before. The spiritual and the animal get so much more sharply divided in hours of encounter, taking possession of the body by swift turns....

TO THE MASTER OF MARLBOROUGH

5 October 1915

I have just time (or rather paper, for that is at present more valuable than time) enough to send a reply to your welcome letter which arrived with the bacon. The chess players are no longer waiting so infernal long between their moves. And the patient pawns are all in movement, hourly expecting further advances—whether to be taken or reach the back lines and be queened. 'Tis sweet, this pawn-being: there are no cares, no doubts: wherefore no regrets. The burden which I am sure is the parent of ill-temper, drunkenness and premature old age—to wit, the making up of one's own mind—is lifted from our shoulders. I can now understand the value of dogma, which is the General Commander-in-Chief of the mind. I am now beginning to think that free thinkers should give their minds into subjection, for we who have given our actions and volitions into subjection gain such marvellous rest thereby. Only of course it is the subjection of their powers of will and deed to a wrong master on the part of a great nation that has led Europe into war. Perhaps afterwards, I and my likes will again become indiscriminate rebels. For the present we find high relief in making ourselves soldiers.

I sent a few lines to *The Marlburian* to the memory and praise of Sidney Woodroffe. Now that one looks back, such an end seemed destined. The Woodroffes were a pair in whom every one of however different temperaments and interests seemed to unite to find a friend.

We no longer know what tomorrow may bring. As I indicated, we no longer worry. Only certain it is that the Bosch has started his long way homeward....

TO ARTHUR WATTS

5 October 1915

Just a line—albeit on military ruled paper. It is the eve of our crowning hour.

I am bleached with chalk and grown hairy. And I think exultantly and sweetly of the one or two or three outstandingly admirable meals of my life. One in Yorkshire, in an inn upon the moors, with a fire of logs and ale and tea and every sort of Yorkshire bakery, especially bears me company. And yet another in Mecklenburg-Schwerin (where they are very English) in a farm-house utterly at peace in broad fields sloping to the sea. I remember a tureen of champagne in the middle of the table, to which we helped ourselves with ladles! I remember my hunger after three hours' ride over the country: and the fishing-town of Wismar lying like an English town on the sea. In that great old farm-house where I dined at 3 p.m. as the May day began to cool, fruit of sea and of land joined hands together, fish fresh caught and ducks fresh killed: it was a wedding of the elements. It was perhaps the greatest meal I have had ever, for everything we ate had been alive that morning—the champagne was alive yet. We feasted like kings till the sun sank, for it was impossible to overeat. 'Twas Homeric and its memory fills many hungry hours.

I was interested in your tale of meeting Wells. Yet a man to whom every private incident is legitimate 'copy' I cannot understand.

I can see you amongst your staff of warrior non-combatants: and (with you) both wish you, and wish you not, rid of them. To be able to prove oneself no coward to oneself, will be great, if it comes off: but suppose one finds oneself fail in the test? I dread my own censorious self in the coming conflict—I also have great physical dread of pain. Still, a good edge is given to the sword here. And one learns to be a servant. The soul is disciplined. So much for me. But the good it would do in your case is that it would discipline your liver. The first need of man is health. And I wish it you for your happiness, though somehow I seem to know you more closely when you are fighting a well-fought battle with ill-health.

Adieu! or (chances three to one in favour of the pleasanter alternative) auf wiedersehen! Pray that I ride my frisky nerves with a cool and steady hand when the time arrives. And you don't know how much I long for our next meeting—more even than for the aforementioned meal!

TO PROFESSOR SORLEY

5 October 1915

Many thanks for the letters which arrived with the rations this morning. We are now embarked on a very different kind of life; whether one considers it preferable or otherwise to the previous, depending on one's mood. It is going to be a very slow business, but I hope a steady one. There is absolutely no doubt that the Bosch is now on his way home, though it is a long way and he will have many halts by the wayside. That 'the war may end any year now' is the latest joke, which sums up the situation....

You will have seen that we have suffered by the loss of our chief: also that our battalion has lost its finest officer—otherwise commissioned ranks have been extraordinarily lucky. For the present, rain and dirt and damp cold. O for a bath! Much love to all.

NOTES

The substance of many of these notes is taken from Professor Sorley's notes to *Marlborough and Other Poems*, 5th edition (1922).

p. 30. 'Rain'. First published in *The Marlburian*, 31 October 1912.
Court. The quadrangle at Marlborough College.
sweat. Marlborough slang for 'run'.
Four Miler. Marlborough name for the clump of trees that stood at the fourth milestone on the old Swindon Road.

p. 32. 'A Call to Action'. First published in *The Marlburian*, 31 October 1912.

p. 34. 'A Tale of Two Careers'. First published in *The Marlburian*, 11 November 1912.
kish. A flat cushion which, folded double, served the Marlburians of CHS's time as a book-carrier.
barnes. Marlborough slang for 'trousers'.
forty-cap. Second fifteen football cap.

p. 36. 'Peace'. First published in *The Marlburian*, 19 December 1912.

p. 38. 'The River'. First published in *The Marlburian*, 25 February 1913.

p. 41. 'The Seekers'. First published in *The Marlburian*, 13 March 1913.

p. 43. 'Rooks'. First published in *The Marlburian*, 10 July 1913.

p. 44. 'What You Will'. First published in *The Marlburian*, 10 July 1913.

p. 45. 'Stones'. First published in *The Marlburian*, 28 July 1913.

p. 46. 'East Kennet Church at Evening'. First published in *The Marlburian*, 3 December 1913.

p. 47. 'Rooks II'. First published in *The Marlburian*, 28 July 1913.

p. 49. 'Autumn Dawn'. First published in *The Marlburian*, 9 October 1913.

p. 51. 'Richard Jefferies'. First published in *The Marlburian*, 9 October 1913. Jefferies (1848-1887) was born in the village of Coate (now part of Swindon). Sorley was devoted to Jefferies's books, many of which were written on the hill known as Liddington Castle which overlooks the Kennet Valley to the south and the Vale of the White Horse to the north.

p. 52. 'J.B.' First published in *The Marlburian*, 9 October 1913. *J.B.* i.e. John Bain, a Marlborough classics master, himself a minor poet; he had left Marlborough at the end of the previous term. Like Sorley he was a Scot and the phrase 'toun o' touns' is an echo from one of his verses.

p. 53. 'The Other Wise Man'. First published in '*The Marlburian*, 10 February 1914.

p. 57. 'Marlborough'. The origin of the story in 'II' may be found in Genesis 32.23 - 33.1.

p. 61. 'Whom Therefore We Ignorantly Worship'. Adapted from The Acts of the Apostles, 17.23, 'Whom therefore ye ignorantly worship, him declare I unto you'.

p. 63. 'Brand'. This and the following poem represent Sorley's impressions of these two characters from Ibsen's long verse plays, *Brand* and *Peer Gynt*.

p. 66. 'Deus Loquitur'. i.e. God speaks.

p. 66. 'Le Revenant'. i.e. The Ghost.

p. 70. 'Expectans Expectavi'. First printed in *The Times Literary Supplement*, 28 October 1915.
Expectans Expectavi. i.e. I have waited hopefully.

p. 73. 'To J.B.' This poem was originally sent to John Bain (see note on 'J.B.' above). When he sent it for publication Bain omitted to send 32 lines which he felt were too flattering to him personally; these lines were first published in the Literary Supplement to *The Marlburian* for the Lent Term, 1967. The poem is now published complete from the manuscript for the first time; there are a number of minor corrections from the earlier

printed text.
κ.τ.λ. και τα λοιπα. i.e. etcetera.
ἀοιδος. i.e. minstrel.
ἐρατεινή i.e. lovely.

p. 77. 'In Memoriam'. First published in *The Marlburian*, 24 November 1915.
S.C.W. Sidney Clayton Woodroffe; CHS's contemporary at Marlborough, Woodroffe was killed at Hooge on 30 July 1915.

p. 77. 'When you see millions'. This sonnet, probably CHS's last poem, was found in Sorley's kit sent home from France after his death.

p. 83. *27 January 1913.*
Alexander Paterson. Paterson, later Sir Alexander Paterson (1884-1947) had lectured at Marlborough the previous term.
Across the Bridges. Written by Alexander Paterson (1911).

p. 85. *20 February 1914.*
'Εσπέρα παντα φέρων. i.e. Evening, the bringer of all things.
Vaterland...wiedersehen. i.e. Fatherland, my Fatherland, we shall meet again.

p. 88. *26 July 1914*
Verbindungen. i.e. the 'Corps' students.
Erst, wenn...gelebt. i.e. Only when he has to die on this earth, shall we realize that he has lived here.

p. 88. *10 August 1914.*
A.E. Hutchinson. One of CHS's schoolfriends.
Totschiessen. i.e. Shoot them!
Hopper. i.e. A.J. Hopkinson, one of CHS's schoolfriends. (See the next letter).
Ihr seid ...Jungen. i.e. You must be lads from Hamburg.
feiner Mann. i.e. a good fellow.
Haben Sie...Bier? i.e. Do you have Munich beer?

p. 93. *October 1914.*
Er wandle...Augenblick. Translated in a letter of Sorley's not here reproduced as:

So let him journey through his earthly day,
Mid hustling spirits, go his self-found way,
Find torture, bliss, in every forward stride,
He, every moment still unsatisfied!

p. 96. *March 1915.*

Weltmacht. i.e. world-power.

p. 98. *1 June 1915.*

Arthur Watts. Lektor in English at the university of Jena when CHS was there in mid-1914.

Schottische Sparsamkeit. i.e. Scottish thrift.

Man muss...geniessen. i.e. One must enjoy the passing moment.

Leb' wohl. i.e. Goodbye.

p. 102. *15 July 1915.*

θαυμάσιον ὅσον. i.e. Wonderfully great.

Index of First Lines of Poems